WHAT THEY'RE SAYING

"A real winner! Copies need to be in every library."

—**J.N., MLS**, Public Library Manager

"The author addresses true hot button issues of our century. Must reading!"

—**G.B.D.**, Physician

"David Ray does a magnificent job of tackling awkward topics with sensitivity, compassion, and good old-fashioned common sense. Very useful for readers of all ages including teenagers."

—**L.W.D.**, CPA (retired)

"Covers very difficult subjects with Christian grace and understanding."

—**C.S.P.**, Teacher

"This material is an ideal guidebook for groups and classes."

—**C.E.P.**, Sales Rep

"During thirty-six years as a police officer, criminal defense lawyer, and in the District Attorney's office, I can verify that David Ray is on target."

—**D. D.**, Attorney

"A Big House On Main Street hit close to home. I lived through fourteen Danger Signs in one of the chapters."

—**L.G.J.**, Office Manager

"This book touches on many delicate topics that need to be discussed openly especially in churches, schools, and community organizations."

—**K. W.**, Legal Technician

"Family members, friends, pastors, and Christian educators will also benefit from this book."

—**T. B.**, Housewife

"The chapter about pets was particularly interesting. David Ray accentuates his points with delightful stories."

—**C. S.**, Pet Lover

"The author leaves no doubt that there is hope—always hope—for everyone with a problem."

—**L. R. A.,** young housewife

"I am struck by how full of down-to-earth encouragement is in this book."

—**E.K.E.,** Library References Services

"David Ray is brief enough to be effective."

—**E. H.,** Health Care Specialist

"Very well done."

—**W.G.,** Real Estate Appraiser

"David Ray outlines in-depth thoughts that will have a lasting impact—even for grandmothers like me!"

—**J.W.G.,** Girl Scout Professional (retired)

"Very helpful for anyone who wants to make living a satisfying, growing, joy-filled experience."

—**M.F.B.,** High School Teacher

"These issues need to be dealth with publicly by ministers and in churches. David Ray presents solid ideas in a way that stimulates people to think."

—**W.R.,** Engineer

"Right on track! I appreciate the author's inclusion of prayer and counseling as ways to bring answers to the problems."

—**J.S.,** Author

"Great job! The book is perfect for small groups, as well as individuals."

—**B.C.S.,** Housewife

RECOMMENDED USES

A pastor at one of the largest, most respected churches in his state said that, in addition to individual use, *Secrets Behind Closed Doors* is a valuable resource book for discussion in families, small groups, classes, clubs, and community groups.

IF, AFTER READING THIS BOOK,

you have an experience you would like to share, I'd love to hear from you. I am also eager to get your response about the book itself. Rest assured that I will pay attention, but be sure to identify yourself. For many years, I have made it a point to discard all anonymous correspondence without reading it. Although I would like to answer each person individually, the volume of mail makes it impractical at times. Your understanding is appreciated.

You may contact me at:
David Ray
PO Box 1021
Clinton, MS 39060-1021
E-mail: DRBooks@bellsouth.net

SECRETS BEHIND CLOSED DOORS

SECRETS BEHIND CLOSED DOORS

DAVID RAY

ISBN 13: 978-1-60615-001-6
ISBN 10: 1-60615-001-4
Library of Congress Catalog Card Number: 2008909979

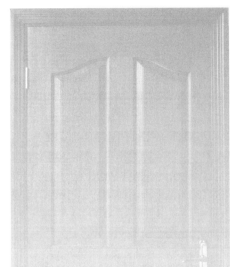

Contents

They Made
the Difference

More than they could possibly know, I am indebted to people in the great Southwest, on the exciting West Coast, and in the charming South whose lives have taught and enriched me over many years.

To young and old from whom I have discovered love, support, stimulation, and acceptance when none of these was deserved.

To students whose fresh thinking and honest, persuasive challenges to worn-out ways continue to move me toward new, although at times, uncomfortable depths in thought, faith—and daily life.

To people of every race, color, culture, and language all over the world whose lives have shown me that there is a common thread that runs through all of us, connecting each one to the other.

All have contributed to this book.

Also to Mary Frances Bowling, Nora Brunson, Anne Hodges and Martha Power whose timely suggestions and assistance have increased the possibilities that the book will be more beneficial to readers. And Robert Davis without whose technical skills in such an age of technology I would have been as lost as an orphaned nomad in the Sahara Desert.

To each, to all—
thank you.

First Word—
The Beginning

Many books start with an idea, but not this one.

It began with people like they were—moral, spiritual, social, emotional, psychological sores, warts, cancers and all—just like they were, where they were. People of all ages and from all walks of life—believers and non-believers, the churched and the un-churched, non-traditionalists, as well as folk rooted in traditional Judeo-Christian values. I had only one aim—to help them get from where they were to where I believed they could be.

The reasons that names have been changed will become obvious.

Although issues are not new, they have become much more prevalent, certainly more public, in this century. In the past, a common response to some of the more sensitive ones has been all the way from infamous R's—ranting, railing and raving—to the dreadful S—silence—to untamed controversy, to irrational confrontation.

We all recognize the increasing pervasiveness of issues in society, but the willingness of communities, churches, and many folks to acknowledge the extent of these issues has been slower than the flow of molasses on a cold winter day. Maybe one of the reasons is a pious reluctance.

While reading, you will come across ideas like: Seven Step Emancipation Plan, the I-Would-Like-For-It-to-Be Principle, Twenty-one Day Forward into the Past Plan, Covenant Connection, Last Step—Next Step Plan, the Blame Game Shuffle, Twelve Ways to Respond to a Gay Family Member or Friend without Compromising Convictions, Forsaking Faith, Surrendering Sanity and Giving Up Goodwill, and Nay to I Am Alive to Dive—Yea to I Am Alive to Thrive.

Chapters include an A.P.S. (Author's Postscript), specialty sections, and street responses to on-line surveys and questionnaires I conducted that will advance a more down-to-earth understanding of the issues.

When considering the issues, the great challenge for a person like me is to be honest, straight up, and true to value principles *without* being an agent of condemnation. I try to live up to that calling.

For hundreds of millions of people, pets are part of the family circle—including mine—so a faith-based approach to them and the environment is important. Annette felt the same way. You will find it in this book.

Reviewers say that people who don't have issues discussed in the book also need to read it, because the steps and principles outlined are workable in every life. By applying them, you will notice a substantial difference in your own world and the worlds of your closest contacts. At the same time, I believe you will rise to your possibilities, while helping others to do the same.

—**David Ray**

Introduction:
A Big House
on Main Street

He didn't project the appearance of a sinister, devil-like monster—you know the dark, sunken, penetrating eyes that could bore a hole through your bones.

To tell the truth, his warm personality and contagious smile would disarm a demon.

That's the kind of person who put Jill behind closed doors in the big house—fourteen rooms in all—on Main Street.

Every room in the big house on Main Street is occupied by people who differ from those in the other rooms. Just like you'd expect, there is a door leading in and out of each room.

People in a big house are going through various life experiences, so every room represents a particular reality for its occupant(s). Yet the impact of their experiences has widespread implications, not only for the ones going through them, but also their families, friends, neighbors, and communities. In fact, millions—many millions—of people are affected by them.

Funny thing about those doors in the big house on Main Street—they swing in and out. Still, many who live in the big house try to keep them closed . . . tight.

Now, you have the setting for the book you are about to read.

Look close into the big house on Main Street. See if you find a loved one, friend, neighbor, or workmate.

Maybe yourself.

Don't be surprised if a fellow church member lives there.

Rise, let us go from this place.
—Jesus (Matt. 26:46)

Chapter One

*"I'm still walking—
but I might as well be dead."*

Tom—Gave Up on Life

Life plays tricks on people at times—at least, some think it does. Tom was one of them.

Not long after entering his productive years, Tom became a follower of Christ and was accepted into God's forgiven family. His practical interest in spiritual things was noticeable. A person could tell that he really enjoyed serving as a teacher and youth advisor at church. He also delighted in activities with others who had families in his age range. Certain that believers could make a positive difference in the community, he was actively involved in programs like Little League and the Kiwanis Club.

Tom was an energetic worker and an entrepreneur. "One who wasn't shy about taking calculated risks," a friend observed. Others agreed that those were some reasons he succeeded in business.

Life was very good for Tom and his family; it was a joy to be around him. Then the economy went into a nosedive. Conditions for him changed. One was a business failure.

"I couldn't stop it," Tom moaned.

People respond to developments like these in different ways; some make matters worse. Vodka was one of Tom's coping mechanisms.

It's not as obvious, he thought. *People can't smell it.*

Another casualty was his marriage. By that time, he had begun to think and behave like it didn't make any difference whether he lived or died. "I'm still walking," Tom lamented, "but I might as well be dead." Oh, don't get me wrong—he never would have taken his own life, but he acted as if he would not mind death.

If Hattie Vose Hall had a person in mind, it could have been someone like Tom when she wrote,

> Gone is the Builder's temple,
> Crumpled into the dust;
> Low lies each stately pillar,
> Food for consuming rust.[1]

With the proliferation of opportunities these days, it seems paradoxical to me when a person lives withdrawn into feelings that his life is like the lunar surface—dry and desolate. As with Tom, maybe times like these are brought on by circumstances beyond one's control.

Maybe not.

Either way, more serious problems could develop when there is failure to respond in appropriate ways. Life could spiral out of control and the drive to survive could go limp.

Six Guidebook Answers—
There's a Way over This Mountain

1. Renounce the serf demon.

In the feudal system hundreds of years ago, a serf was one bound to a master's land. His servitude went with the property and whoever owned it, even when the property changed hands. He had no power to make choices. He was a slave to his condition—serfdom.

Spurred on by adversity, it is common for a serf-like attitude to bind a person to reverses by enticing him into thinking that he is powerless or without sufficient resources to deal with whatever has happened or is happening in life. A prominent man experienced it after he tumbled from his prestigious, influential position. Later, his daughter described his condition saying, "It is as if he is fading himself away."

But a marvel of the human spirit is proof that a person may be subjected to challenging developments, yet, does *not* have to sink into destruction because of it. If this were not true, many of the great people whose lives enrich us would have remained in bondage to abnormal conditions in their lives.

For instance, the prolific inventor Thomas Edison, suffered from deafness. He experienced 90 percent hearing loss. Likewise Helen Keller—blindness. Also my friend, Jim Fuhrman, who contracted a horrid degenerative disease, yet he still managed a productive career at the California Institute of Technology, although totally dependent on a caregiver for the last fifteen years.

Nay to "I Am Alive to Dive!"

I have seen the chilling phrase, "born to lose," tattooed on gang members. That phrase might strike you, like it has me, as being so pagan and so "unlike my sort of person." But think about this before dismissing it altogether: When we acknowledge that reverses in life are too big to manage, we are also buying into a blatant lie straight from the depths of the deceiver. Accepting that lie will make a setback a permanent change instead of a momentary stumble.

This concept has been tagged, "I am alive to dive," which is a child of "born to lose." "I have life so that I can fail" is another way to describe it. When dressed in nice, comfortable, acceptable, religious terms like, "What has happened or is happening is God's will," the notion about failure and problems becomes more palatable. No, it isn't—unless God is a failure! Unceremoniously, boot those thoughts out of your life! Loud and clear, say nay to "I am alive to dive." And yea to . . .

"I AM ALIVE TO THRIVE!"

A follower of Jesus made it plain that, in pure goodness and infinite wisdom, God put two grand plans in place for you before you were born, even before the world was made (Eph. 1:3–5). One, you are chosen to be a member in full standing of the Lord's forgiven family with all rights and privileges that come with it. Two, you are destined to be successful in life.

Neither plan has changed.

Failure to experience either plan is no fault of the plan or the architect behind it.

Affirm Your Destiny

Keep the following sentences in your heart and at your fingertips. Believe them, accept them, repeat them often. *Don't let feeling get in the way*. Repeat them until you can believe and accept them.

- I was born to be—a winner.
- I can become what I was born to be—a winner.
- I will become what I was born to be—a winner.
- Today, by the grace of God, I am becoming what I was born to be—a winner (Phil. 4:13).

2. Treat adversity as a curve.

Curves on a highway always start somewhere, always go somewhere, and always end somewhere. I have also noticed that at times they follow one after the other. Still, there is a point where the road straightens.

People who travel along California's Highway 1 in the Carmel-Big Sur area cannot help but marvel at the majestic scenery and spectacular seascapes. They feel their hearts pounding as they creep along the edge of cliffs, trying to glimpse the waves smashing craggy rocks below them. They get goose bumps during those hairpin turns. Eventually, though, the curves stop.

Contrary conditions in life create the illusion that no end of the curves is in sight. But like that road from Carmel to Big Sur they always do. And just like that road, adverse developments never have *forever* engraved on them—never! Ever! That is, unless a person allows them to continue or, worse yet, unconditionally surrenders to them.

3. Brag about a good thing.

It's impossible to talk failure and then succeed, to talk weakness and then be strong, to talk fear and then be courageous, to talk doubt and then believe.

I listened while someone complained, "There is nothing good in my life."

In an effort to help, others volunteered suggestions like, "Enlarge your social circle." "Channel your energy into changing your life." "Get your mind off of your problems."

Good advice, I thought, but one member of the group didn't mince words when she declared, "That isn't true! There is something good in your life!" And she was right.

This very moment, there is something good in every person's life—your life!

Set aside a Brag Time and start with one positive feature of your life. Stay on it until another one comes to mind.

Continue Brag Time every day for forty days.

I am not so naïve as to think bragging will overcome the bad stuff, but it will open the door for you to recognize favors that adversity is hiding from you. Brag Time will grow the power of positives and shrink the strength of negatives. It will also help maintain a more wholesome perspective on what is going on inside you, to you, around you, in the community, and in the world.

4. Own what is no longer owned.

I am thinking of a coin I call *possessions*. Like all coins, it has two sides. One side represents the need to own what a person has. I have met people who don't own their stuff. Favored with an overflow of things, they have an almost insatiable appetite for more. In this condition, possessions possess them. The name of their demon and slave master, is "Enough Is Never Enough." They are mastered, not masters.

I have also known people who live on the other side of the coin. That side represents the need to own what a person *doesn't* own. The lack or loss of possessions can possess a person just as demonically as an overflow of wealth. Furthermore, enslavement to lack or loss of possessions is just as debilitating as enslavement to many possessions because its victims fall captive to another demon named "Not Enough."

Failure to own meager, reduced, or lost possessions also leaves a person in tattered emotional and spiritual rags.

Money may not be as plentiful as it once was. Comforts you recently enjoyed have disappeared. Like pesky mosquitoes, thoughts about more prosperous yesterdays come from the north, south, east, and west. Yearnings to return to those good old days are ravenous.

Enough of What Is Not!

Agree that you've had enough of what is not and start to do something about *what is*. The word that comes to mind is "contentment." Another follower of Jesus wrote about living temporarily in either prosperity or poverty: "I have learned the secret of making it whether I have a lot or a little" (Phil. 4:11–12).

To own what is not now owned:

- Aim your sights on whatever is now available, not on what is unavailable.
- Put what you now have to the best use possible.
- Concentrate on one thought at a time, and direct your attention away from things you do not have.
- *Apply* yourself to activities that could usher in brighter, more prosperous days.

5. Adopt a herd strategy.

Go out of your way to have conversations with individuals who have successfully maneuvered through a similar time in life. Believe me, a person like that is within access! And there's probably more than one.

Let Someone Be Good to You—and Himself!

Strength from example and the influence of triumph are valuable helps that no one needs to go without. Besides, when someone is good to others, he is also good to himself. Give someone the opportunity to be good to himself by helping you.

6. Deploy Hope Prayers.

I have observed five approaches common in the prayers of people who think that life is beating them up or that they are a punching bag for circumstances outside of their control.

- *Nope Prayers* drip with gloom and drown in doom. ("God, I'm not sure why I'm praying because there doesn't seem to be a realistic answer for me.")
- *Grope Prayers* grasp for straws. ("I don't have any idea, Lord, how this could happen to me, and I don't have the foggiest idea where I'll wind up.")
- *Float Prayers* are usually an avalanche of petitions, void of focus and smothered by confusion. ("I'm asking for a lot, God. Maybe you'll answer one of them. I sure hope so.")
- *Dope Prayers* challenge good sense by consisting mostly of commands and directives to God. ("I know what is best for me, so, Lord, do this, and that, and the other.")
- *Mope Prayers* are soaked in self-pity. ("Poor me, God! How could something like this happen to me—to ME, of all people?")

What is needed, however, are *Hope Prayers*—honest, straight forward, one-on-one talks with the Almighty. They have some unmistakable, defining characteristics such as being open to God the way you are and as much as you know; a readiness to trust that what you need will be available when you need it; and a willingness to believe for a turnaround. Remember, these kind of prayers are accompanied with action to bring it about.

Bless yourself with Hope Prayers not once or twice, but each day, especially for the next forty days. Begin the day by giving God control over the experiences that await you during the day. Anyone who does this audibly finds that sound of the words adds a note of reality to the thoughts and ideas.

I recall the person who told me that an assignment like this was a lifesaver:

> God, both of us know this is a tough time for me. I refuse to believe that I am alone today. I refuse to believe that I have to carry the load by myself today. I refuse to believe that I am powerless. I know that I need Your help to make it through this day. I accept it. Amen.

Remember Tom? Did he do this?

No.

He wound up on a dead end road named "What's the Use." A perception of diminished resources set in. Like a meltdown in the face of an advancing army of terrorists, his will to live gradually, steadily evaporated until he caved in.

Millions of others have been in situations similar to Tom's, and worse. Yet they have demonstrated that they are "alive to thrive." Tom should have and would have, but . . .

According to the Gospel, the fullness of life is available to everyone (John 10:10). Tom's drive to survive and thrive could have been revived, but it wasn't. Jesus assured us that "all things are possible for the one who believes" (Mark 9:23). Tom could have flourished again, but he didn't.

Tom died before his time.

I know.

He was my brother.

According to the doctor, the cause of death was organ failure. Medically, I suppose he was right. But I'm convinced that the true cause went deeper. I think Tom's loss of the will to live was fatal. At his death, were the tears shed on earth felt in heaven?

They could have been.

A. P. S.
(Author's Postscript)

Sir James Matthew Barrie, the Scottish author and playwright, observed that life is a diary in which we intend to write one story, but instead write another, and that our most humbling hour is when we compare the story actually written with what we had hoped to write.[2]

The life story you are writing is inseparably linked to the depth of the conviction that you are alive to thrive because the strength of that conviction affects your actions and reactions when circumstances try to convince you that you are alive to dive.

If you aren't convinced, deeply convinced, that God has planned success for you, you won't meet setbacks with confidence that there is a way to cope, that you can find it, and that you can conquer. Instead of the divine way, the setbacks will have their way and you will lose.

What if it were true that you were born to lose?

Or to win some of the time and lose some of the time?

Or to live life on less than a full cup?

For a horrifying moment, follow that trail to where it winds up. You are a random coincidence, not the orchestration of the divine hand. You are a mistake. Fate, not faith (yours) and faithfulness (God's), determines the quality of your life. Disorder rather than order has the upper hand. Circumstances trump persons. Life discriminates and plays favorites. Existence without purpose is the norm.

Now here's the truth: No condition, even the most adversarial one, erases the divine reality that

- You were born to succeed.
- You are alive to thrive.
- Your destiny is to know God and enjoy Him now and forever.

Discussion Room

Agree	Disagree	
☐	☐	If the level of life with meaning and purpose can be compared to a tank of gasoline in a car, it's OK to live on ¼ tank.
☐	☐	No one has a full tank
☐	☐	It's irresponsible to think someone can live on a full tank, even a three quarters tank.
☐	☐	Everyone has ups and downs in life.
☐	☐	If Tom had truly trusted God, he wouldn't have let his problems get the upper hand.
☐	☐	It isn't possible for a person to be a winner all of the time.
☐	☐	God has to be behind some problems, otherwise they wouldn't happen.
☐	☐	The root of Tom's problem was money—not enough of it.
☐	☐	Some people are "alive to thrive" and others are "alive to dive."
☐	☐	Contentment is a sanctimonious excuse for failure and lack of achievement.
☐	☐	God uses adversity to accomplish His purposes.
☐	☐	To change a reality, a person has to cope with the existing reality.
☐	☐	Tom's problems were God's will.
☐	☐	Love of possessions causes problems.
☐	☐	If Tom only had more faith, the outcome would have been different.
☐	☐	When you can't do anything about something, the best thing to do is admit you can't do anything about it and accept it.

Seventeen Characteristics I've Noticed in People Who Are on the Way to Losing the Will to Live

- Increasingly perplexed about the adverse development—"Why is it happening?"
- More personally directed questions—"Why is it happening to *me*?"
- Confusion about their response—"What can I do?" "Is there anything I can do?"
- Spreading belief that life is unfair—"I don't deserve this."
- Persecution complex—"Something or somebody bad has me targeted."
- Animosity—"It's me vs. 'that' and 'that' is using me for a punching bag."
- Submission to circumstances—"They're stronger than I am."
- Dependence on external stimulants—"I need this so that I can forget my troubles."
- Embarrassment and humiliation—"I can't afford what I used to enjoy."
- Envy—"What have others done to be so much better off than me?"
- Withdrawal—"I don't want or need to be around others. They're not going through what I'm going through."
- Church dropout—"Why should I continue? It would be hypocritical of me."
- Resentment—"God, you could do something about this, if you would."
- Sidelined faith—"It's not working for me."
- Collapse of self-esteem—"I'm a nobody now."
- Decline toward depression—"I'm so overwhelmed."
- Lost hope—"There's no answer. Things would be better if I were dead."

Prayer to Thrive

Everlasting Father, Source of the victorious way, visit those who still breathe, walk and talk, yet are in a death-doesn't-matter mode. Help them to acknowledge that You are at hand to be strength to them and that You are ready to encircle them with sustaining mercies.

Clear their vision to see further than the problems they are experiencing at the moment. Point the eyes of their souls away from themselves. In grace, establish the hope within them that will carry them forward.

And, mighty Lord, persuade them to let You do something good for them through others. Inspire them to begin rising to their possibilities today. In the spirit of the One who offers healing for ruptures in life. Amen.

Good News

There remains great opportunity for having a useful life and doing good work . . . I will put my law in your mind and I will write it on your heart. I will be your God and you will be my person (1 Cor. 16:9; Jer. 31:33).

Chapter Two

Could she forgive him—really?
Should she? Why would she? How did she?

Jill, Someone Special—and Abused

Ages six through eleven are years of innocence, right? They should be filled with school, friends, slumber parties, endless gab-fests full of chatter flowing at speeds of 100 mph with gusts up to 150. And let's not forget soccer, spelling bees, and church activities, if a believing family.

James Russell Lowell referred to growing-up years as the time to see children as God's apostles of love and hope and peace.[3]

Not so for Jill, at least not as much as most kids experience. Her childhood years included abuse at the hands of a neighbor. But more than a neighbor—a family friend and member of the same church! Not the sinister, conniving, devil-like monster we'd imagine. His warmth, smiles, and attentiveness would disarm any demon.

Like many other victims, Jill didn't say anything while the abuse continued. She was one of the 90 percent of cases that go unreported. Besides, the abuse stopped when the neighbor moved to another city.

The trauma she experienced went into remission for awhile. Then fresh out of college and preparing to begin graduate school, those experiences attacked her wellbeing like a party of ancient Vikings plundering villages along Canada's coastline.

From one direction, haunting memories. From another, guilt, anxiety, and self-recrimination. Her turmoil was similar to ones described by the author who wrote,

> With what anguish of mind I remember my childhood . . .
> Are things I remember with tears in my eyes,
> As memory reverts—
> And I gag at the thought of that horrible well.[4]

Jill felt the experiences as if they were happening again. Thank God, she did not fall into problems common to other victims of abuse—alcoholism, drug addictions, eating disorders, or depression. At times, though, she lay awake wondering if the damage to her soul was beyond repair. Occasionally, it seemed like the stain on her life was irreversible.

"Can I move away from the devastation?" Jill asked. "Where was I at fault?"

During my efforts to help victims like Jill, it became very clear that abuse is more than sexual. I began to see it is a frontal assault on the grandest gift one has been afforded—the gift of person made in God's image.

This kind of abuse is a raw transgression of the physical, emotional, social, and spiritual rights granted with the gift of person and one of the ugliest violations of God's purpose for two people—the one abused and the abuser. The damage it may cause to their families and communities is akin to a category five emotional, social, physical, and spiritual hurricane.

As in Jill's case, effects of abuse sometimes go into hiding—a sleeper effect—then break out years later.

Six Guidebook Answers—
the Road to Recovery

Recovery Rule 1: Face it

More lies here than meets the eye. Facing any overwhelming event—such as abuse in Jill's case—involves honest recognition: It is what it is and what happened really happened.

An abuse victim who recovered told me, "Because the one who did it wasn't a vicious, despicable sort of person, I tried to put some lipstick on it and dress it up (instead of calling it 'abuse'). It was what it was—abuse, and not something with a nicer name. The one who did it was what he was—a deviant individual who acted in a predatory way even though he was a respected, successful person. And it was done to *me*."

Nothing changes the reality of what abuse is and the nature of the person who abuses.

Severity of abuse is also included in recognition. Attempts like these to sugar coat it have no healing value:

"Oh, he or she [the perpetrator] isn't all that bad."
"It isn't really as ugly as you think."
"He or she didn't mean it the way you see it."
"You're taking it the wrong way."

Permanent Impact Can Be Changed!

Although the reality of abuse cannot be changed, the permanent impact on a person can be. Face abuse straight on and underscore happen*ed—past* tense. Effects may linger, but their influence deserves to die.

Recovery Rule 2: Disclose it

Disclosure is an important step in healing and affects at least two people who are most directly affected—the abused and the abuser, plus society. The abused person needs to effectively deal with what happened in order to overcome it. The abuser needs to be held accountable for his or her actions. Otherwise the likelihood of change is only a pipe dream.

Report the Abuse as Soon as Possible

Professionals working with victims have found that the trauma caused by abuse is usually reduced by reporting it and that short-term and long-term consequences for the one abused are less severe the *quicker* the abuse is disclosed.[5]

Dismiss any second thoughts about not making abuse known and do not allow any wiggle room for who or what the abuser may be. Friend, neighbor, or family member, a well-known or unknown person, a younger person, an older person, a well-connected or unconnected or disconnected person, someone with meager or many possessions—none of these should make any difference.

Talk to someone (other than the abuser, of course) who may make a difference. For example, a parent, brother, sister, close friend, teacher, health professional, minister, or even the police. Don't allow excuses to interfere such as:

> "I don't want to ruin his life."
> "What good will it do?"
> "I want to put it behind me."
> "How will bringing it up now help?"
> "Who would believe me?"

Back up for a moment. Doesn't abuse deserve to be met with zero tolerance? According to counselors, it is a major problem in many nations—much greater than statistics indicate. Tolerance only coddles and inflates the problem. From experience, I have long been comfortable with the view that the best interests of the most people are served when abuse is met by a *total absence of sympathy*. Worries about consequences for the abuser can be tabled in favor of wholeness.

Then there is forgiveness to consider.

Does forgiveness remove consequences?

One of the first laws of accountability that children should be taught is this: Every act has a consequence. Consequences to an abuser should be real. So should forgiveness. However, forgiveness does *not* wipe out potential legal and social ramifications of the transgression.

Not only does disclosure have beneficial effects on personal healing, it holds the abuser accountable and may do him a favor he will never forget. It may be the most influential factor in pushing him toward an unmasked confrontation with the awful act and jolt him into starting on the road to becoming a new person.

One man said that when a relative reported him to the police, he was filled with rage and overwhelmed by humiliation. "But," he confessed, "it was the beginning of the turn-around I needed." As a bonus benefit, "It also spared others from becoming victims."

Recovery Rule 3: Place it

Put blame for abuse where it belongs—on the *abuser*. Perpetrators offer an endless litany of "I'm not to blame" explanations.

"I was abused."
"I didn't have the upbringing I needed."
"It's okay within my family circle."
"She or he asked for it."
"The harm is overstated."
"No one is perfect."
"Everyone does something wrong—this is one of mine."
"It isn't committed in violence."
"He or she (the abused) wouldn't get attention, if it weren't for me."
"A sin is a sin—this one is no worse than any other sin."
"It's only among us, and I have a right."
"I was born a sinner, and I will die a sinner."

Endless explanations will not dissolve a snippet of guilt or remove the slightest wink of responsibility. To apply the gist of an old spiritual song, it's not my brother, it's not my sister, it's not my parents, grandparents, uncle, aunt, environment, society, or my DNA, but me, standing in need.

The culprit in abuse cases is the person who commits abuse. No reason is credible enough to bring on abuse and no argument is persuasive enough to excuse it.

Stop Blaming Yourself!

Recovery Rule 4: Surround it

Children and adults who were abused agree that support of family members and others outside of the family circle are two of the most critical contributions to their recovery. Surround yourself, or let others surround you, with the assistance needed to more adequately deal with the aftermath of the abuse, including professional help, a support group, trusted friends at church, and individuals who really care.

I know someone who wanted to keep private what happened. "I was so ashamed," she explained, but her plan did not work. The by-myself-approach can create more hazards on the path of healing than a mine-laden war zone.

Let Others Help You!

Remember, God has tapped someone on the shoulder to walk the road to recovery with you, and possibly more than one person. Also keep in mind that in different ways, the help someone gives may help the one giving it as much as the one receiving it. This is one of the marvelous ways through which God successfully works in the lives of two people—the giver and the receiver.

Recovery Rule 5: Pace it

Rarely is healing from abuse instantaneous, therefore, think of it not as a hundred-yard dash, but a hundred-mile marathon run a step at a time. Don't be surprised if, at times, it is one step forward and two steps backward, or three steps ahead and one step toward the rear, or a step sideways and a step back-ways.

Seldom is recovery accomplished in giant leaps forward. Remind yourself that the size of the step is less important than the direction in which the step is taken. Like any recovery process, healing has a starting point. The starting point is where you are, the way you are, with whatever feelings you have.

Delay in Starting the
Process Also Delays the Benefits

Recovery Rule 6: Grace it

Previously, I mentioned that the support of family members and others is critical to recovery. The American Psychological Association reports two additional ingredients: high self-esteem and spirituality.[6] Both are affected by grace, which means divine favor.

You are highly favored. God holds you in great value and offers you life and wellbeing now. Your significance to your Maker is not a single speck less than it was before the abuse. Never at any time, nor for any reason, has your importance been lessened in God's eyes. At this very moment, you are truly the apple of his eye.

You Are Fully Loved!

This means that God cannot love you now any more than He already does because His divine love for you now, where you are, the way you are, is perfect. Nothing can be added to this perfection to make it more perfect.

Did Jill deal with her abuse demon and defeat it?

Yes!

One of the most telling moments in her recovery was the day she contacted the abuser and said, "I forgive you."

He was taken back.

After composing himself, he asked, "Why?"

"Because," Jill started with a spontaneous four point answer,

"It's what I think God wants me to do."

"I need to do it."

"You need for me to do it."

"And I need for you to know that I know you need for me to do it."

She finished graduate studies and began a fine career. She also is blessed with a great family. Like all parents should, Jill and her husband have worked together to teach their children about abuse, ways to recognize it, and helps by which to avoid it.

An outcome like Jill's is possible for anyone in the jaws of abuse of any kind—sexual, verbal, emotional, physical—any kind. How can I be so sure? "With God no thing (and no one) is impossible" (Luke 1:37).

"Thank the Lord!" Jill's family exclaimed.

So did the abuser, who did an about face.

During the process, I assured Jill's family and influential friends that they could be instrumental in her healing. They were encouraged to offer prayers like: *Lord, bless Jill with the awareness of Your closeness to guide her to wholeness. Show me how to be a person she needs at this time. Amen.*

One of my favorite affirmations of faith repeated by millions of followers of Jesus each week includes, *I believe in the Holy Spirit.* I am confident that every time those words are spoken, we declare that there is a mighty God who is able and willing to enter the human personality and change it.

An abuser is changeable, too. I know. I've seen it happen—for good. I challenged the family and friends, as well as Jill, to also pray for the abuser.

> *Forgiving Lord, help him to face his transgression head-on. Shake his soul with the desire to change and make any amends possible. May he see that the door to You is still open and that the invitation to redeemed and restructured life remains in effect, even for him. Amen.*

Like I said, he did an about face—a change which inflicted hurt on the devil.

A lot of hurt!

That also made me glad.

God, too.

What makes me so certain?

He was the One behind it!

A. P. S.
(Author's Postscript)

According to Dr. Shanta Dube and colleagues, approximately one in six boys are abused in the United States and Canada before they reach sixteen years of age.[7] The count is probably underestimated because as many as a third of abused children do not remember the abuse when they become adults.

Information from the U. S. Department of Health & Human Services reveals the extent of the problem in this century by reporting that as many as six million were abused during a twelve month period.[8] However, children and youth are not the only ones targeted for abuse.

People of all ages, both male and female, on all socioeconomic levels, from all races and cultures are susceptible to it—and are guilty of it. For instance, a healed abuser proudly celebrating more than twenty years of "glorious freedom from slavery" was a prominent and affluent person in heartland America.

Usually an abuser takes advantage of some position of power, perceived or real, to use as the platform from which to force or gain entry into encounters. But the power element is deeper than a position. Abusers often want to possess power, show power, and prove how powerful they think they are.

The findings of Dr. Jim Hopper, Harvard Medical School and Massachusetts General Hospital, are dependable. From years of experience and research, he has made these helpful conclusions:[9]

- Many of those who were abused as children have periods of amnesia followed by delayed recall—like Jill.
- Even the most diligent family members or other caregivers are not always able to protect children from painful experiences.
- In itself, abuse does *not* doom a person to a life of failure and problems.
- Every abused person must find ways to cope with feelings and fallout generated by painful experiences.

- An abused person who blames and shames himself could very well cause more damage to himself than the abuse itself.
- Furthermore, abuse is not always confined to intimate activity. Self-exposure, an oversized passion for seeing sexual objects or activities, and pornography deserve the label of abuse.

Discussion Room

Agree	Disagree	
☐	☐	If her parents had been more attentive, Jill wouldn't have suffered abuse.
☐	☐	Too much hoopla surrounds this subject.
☐	☐	Actually, the only thing needed to overcome abuse is a stronger faith.
☐	☐	An abuser shouldn't be reported unless he or she is a habitual offender. Everyone deserves another chance.
☐	☐	Jill should have forgiven and forgotten the entire mess much earlier in her life.
☐	☐	If God is in control, healing should be instantaneous.
☐	☐	Someone who has been abused for a long time will never get over it.
☐	☐	I think I could tell when a person is being abused.
☐	☐	Get real. There are abusers who can't help themselves. The proclivity for it is part of their genetic make-up.
☐	☐	For some, the urge is so strong that they are powerless to stop it.
☐	☐	Someone must have realized that Jill was being abused, yet didn't do anything.
☐	☐	The truth of the matter is—and no matter what she claimed—it was impossible for Jill to completely forgive her abuser.

Agree	Disagree	
☐	☐	Everyone should let some of the pure splendor of his or her value to God rub off on him or her every day.
☐	☐	Everyone could believe that he or she is special—very special

Indicators That Can Give an Abusive Person Away

- Patterns of behavior that cause you second and third thoughts.
- Inclinations that make you have uneasy feelings.
- Lack of respect for wholesome physical, social, and emotional boundaries, such as tickling, touching, hugging, kissing, and horseplay when the person does not want or welcome the attention.
- Tendency to share information and activities with children and youth that would normally be reserved for adults.
- Private, unexplained get-togethers with children and youth.
- Excessive time with children or youth rather than one's own age group, for no particular reason.
- Unusual generosity with children or youth, more special outings with them than is reasonable, and frequent gifts when there is no special occasion.

A Few Telltale Signs of Abuse

- Sleeplessness and abnormal fears for which an explanation is not obvious.
- Loss of appetite, irrational eating changes, and difficulties eating and swallowing.
- Uncharacteristic swings in moods such as isolation, secrecy, anger, insecurity, and phobias.
- Sicknesses that seem to have no causes or cannot be diagnosed.

- Abnormal loss of concentration; scatterbrain without having been scatterbrained in the past.
- New and stronger resistance to bathing, use of toilet, or taking clothes off at appropriate times.
- Destructive, depleted concept of self—tends to see oneself as dirty, nasty, repulsive, and excluded.

Freedom for an Abuser Could Include

- Self-report the abuse. (I am aware of one who did. He was indicted, convicted, imprisoned for a time and found his way to life-changing completeness. "My family and friends wouldn't give up on me," he explained.)
- Avoid contact with people most likely to become victims *except* when other believing, abuse-free persons are present. Consider one-on-one exposure like you would AIDS.
- Apply the brakes to urges to touch, taste, feel, and fantasize *starting the moment* the urges begin. Remove yourself from the scene, mingle with more age-appropriate people, and instantly access strength that is beyond what you alone can muster.
- Limit the type of affection shown to people. Make it more age, sex, and occasion specific.
- Open up to professional and group help.
- Let God change you little-by-little each day. You may be tough, but not so tough that the One who made you for the person you could become cannot change you.

Four Characteristics of All Freed Abusers
I Have Known

1. Self-responsibility. They came to the point where they fully accepted responsibility.
2. Clan-effort. They received support and help from others.

3. Professional teamwork. They would not have made it without the input and guidance of people who were trained and smarter than them.
4. Divine-initiative. They sought and accepted intervention of the mighty God who refused to let them down—or off the hook.

Prayer for Recovery

Bountiful Lord, thank You for being available anytime for anyone with any need. Help those who have been abused to understand that the pain they feel is most deeply felt in heaven and to accept the assurance that their tears really do matter to You.

May they receive assurance that You have not rejected them. Grant that they will be embraced by a love that is so invasive that nothing that has happened will blot out its reality. Come to them with new strength to trust dark memories to You.

Enable them, God of deliverance, to believe that destruction caused by abuse can be repaired. Bring more awareness of the possibility for the ugliness they feel to be healed and ability to recognize that the influence of abuse can be lessened.

Supply what they need now to take a step to overcome doubts which have fastened on to their faith, and to begin an experience of freedom from bondage to shame, bitterness, despair, and suspicions about their worth as persons. In the name of the One through whom lives can be turned toward the sunshine. Amen.

Good News

Look! See what love God has given to you that you should be considered a child of God. And so you are—a child of God . . . Re-ignite the gift that God has given to you for God does not give a spirit of cowardice, but of power, love and self-discipline (1 John 3:1–2; 2 Tim. 1:6–7).

Chapter Three

"If we weren't made the way we are, why are we the way we are?"

Three Friends— Sexual Preference Different from Mine

The capacity to enjoy sexual experience is God-given, so there's no need to treat it like an unmentionable. It should, however, be considered respectfully, discreetly, and reverently.

Of all creation, it seems that humans are most favored with a unique ability to experience the pleasures achieved through intimacy. The thrill of an exclusive and special oneness, a deeper dimension of meaning, achievement of emotional fulfillment, and an increase of spiritual strength are ours when we give and receive love with another person.

Dr. David Osborne at Mayo Clinic underscored the importance of sex when he said that healthy sexual relationships can positively affect all aspects of a person's life including physical health and self-esteem.[10]

But giving and receiving love with someone brings up the topic of sexual preference. Using the word *orientation*, the American Psychological Association has defined it as an "enduring emotional, romantic, sexual, or affectional attraction to another person."[11]

For the giving and receiving of love to be the most gratifying and satisfying, parameters are necessary. That shouldn't raise any eyebrows. All of life has parameters for optimal function. When a person does not function within boundaries, he or she abandons responsibility. Detached from responsibility, intimate experiences leave a person incomplete—if not wasted.

This brings me to three very likeable friends who were gay, or thought they were.

Putting aside arguments over whether their inclination was perceived or real, caused by surroundings, upbringing, genetic or hormonal factors, or plain old depraved human nature, there was no doubt that they were attracted to persons of the same sex.

Forces at work within them seemed undeniable. From most indications, the drive appeared to be overwhelming and their urges had an irrepressible side to them.

Let's take a closer look under the skin of my friends.

For one, the splendid wonder of life tended to be shaded. Mind you, he was no slouch. He possessed many qualities that would cause you to admire him. Still, he thought that his purpose for being on earth had somehow been twisted. He felt baffled and, at times, seriously overwhelmed.

The other two friends rejoiced in a same-sex lifestyle. They were neither secretive about it nor ashamed of it. They had left the overwhelmed-and-baffled stage when they became convinced that sexual preference is nothing more than an extension of the way people are created.

They were truthful about the way they felt. "If we weren't made the way we are, why are we the way we are? We wouldn't be gay, if we weren't made that way."

You would not find them on the wrong side of the tracks either—both were creative professional people who knew their business.

Meet Six Other Friends

Bewildered Me is also puzzled by his attraction to people of the same sex. The entire situation runs contrary to what he has been taught. And it's made worse since no one else in the family is like him, as far as he knows. He would like—no, more than like, he aches—to be free from it. He fits the description reflected in these lines:

The (person) I am
Hides deep in me,
Beneath the (person)
I seem to be.[12]

No Sweat has worked through the problems as far as he is concerned, and made peace with what he thinks is his sexuality. "Don't sweat it," he argues.

To Each His Own has feelings that are a problem to her. Nevertheless, she has come to the conclusion that for her, it is normal to practice a same-sex lifestyle. "To each his own," she insists.

Embarrassed Me has a family member (could be a friend) who is gay and she is embarrassed—downright humiliated. If the truth were known, she is probably angry enough to think about shutting the person out of her life—and may have done that already.

Holier Than Thee has the goods on this gay thing, beyond a doubt. With Bible in hand, he is positive that "it's sinful, *sinful*, S-I-N-F-U-L! People like that are dirty to the bone. A special place in hell is reserved for them."

Oh Dear Me has a family member (or friend) who is gay, and he's convinced that it is wrong. "But how can I handle it? Is there anything I can do or say that will make any difference really?"

Seven Guidebook Answers— Oh, to Be Free!

1. Be direct—ask "why?"

Anyone active in a gay lifestyle, or who thinks he is gay, or may be gay, does himself one of the biggest favors of his life by asking:

- Did a heterosexual relationship bomb out? Maybe several?
- Has the influence of someone who is impressive, a person I admire, led me into it?
- Do I feel more comfortable with someone of the same sex?

- Has my environment in earlier years tilted me in that direction—a mother or father who, perhaps unknowingly, stimulated thought, talk, and behavior like a person of the opposite sex?
- In younger years, did I suffer abuse?
- At a young age, did I engage in sexual activities—extensively?
- Do I think I get "more bang for my buck" out of a same-sex relationship?
- Did the relationship with my wife or husband lose its shine or disappear?
- When up-close and personal, does there seem to be less conflict with people of the same sex?
- Does there seem to be more freedom in playing the field?
- Do out-of-the-accepted-norm activities seem to be more exciting?
- Do random or anonymous encounters actually meet my need?
- Is the idea of a long-term commitment scary?
- Is the departure from tradition my "cup of tea"?
- Is this another way to move beyond a worn-out faith that hasn't worked for me?

2. Goodbye, butt out argument.

People who are reluctant to address a condition or consider information that disagrees with their views and actions often say, "It's none of your concern, so butt out."

Admittedly, the unchristian way some Christian people deal with the sexual preference issue is enough to wish they would butt out. However, sexual partners and behavior cannot be intelligently or spiritually determined on a standalone basis. The reason is . . .

Connectedness.

"It's no one's concern except mine, or the two of us, so mind your own business" contradicts the connectedness among human beings. Subsequently, it divorces a person from the reality of being.

Let me explain.

From birth, we are part of all who are at that time, all who came before us, and all who follow us. "Connectedness" is the tie that binds everyone to the very substance of who he or she is as a deliberate, creative act of God *and* to everyone else who also is a deliberate, creative act of God.

Each person is unique. In a special, real, and exciting sense, every person can say, "I am me and more. I am all others who are at the very time I am and more. I am all who preceded me last week, last month, last year, the last decade, the last century, for generations, even thousands of years and more."

Something else unusually marvelous about connectedness is its assurance that we are endowed with basic equalities even prior to birth including the essential opportunities necessary to experience a fuller measure of life. I'm convinced that the ancient believer had something of it in mind when he wrote, "You, O Lord, created my inmost being; you knit me together in my mother's womb . . . I am wonderfully made" (Ps. 139:13–14, NIV).

You Have Connectedness—You Are in Connection!

So the way you are and the way you live make a difference—a *big* difference.

3. Bury the isolation hatchet.

Stanley Eitzen, a well-known and respected social scientist, lectures about a type of isolation which shows itself in "individuals separated from neighbors, co-workers, and family members." He insists that causes include frequent moves from place to place, numerous job changes, divorce, more new technologies than can be readily absorbed, less visiting with neighbors, both parents working outside the home, too much time spent watching TV (not to mention, may I add, the Internet and how it is used behind closed doors during leisure hours) and the pressures of time.[13]

Dr. Robert Levine, a prominent psychologist, adds that alienation, anonymity, and isolation cause people to feel less responsible for the way they act.[14] Isolation also has influence in the arena of sexual preference and the behavior associated with it. The answer for it which I discuss here is a cousin of #2, yet, different in that it joins

Relatedness

with connectedness to refute the notion that choice of sexual partners and behavior are strictly private matters that have nothing—zilch, nada, zip—to do with anybody else.

That's isolationism. Bury it—or be buried by it!

You see, if sexual partnership concerned no one except the individual, it would separate preference and behavior from the other functions of being a person and from living in a family, community, and society of other persons.

Moreover, it would nullify the impact that being a person has on preference and behavior and, as a consequence, thwart the power—at least, some of it—in being a person.

Relatedness insists that there is a pivotal role for faith, family, community, and society. It is certain that others deeply matter. It is a guarantee that a person does not have to remain the way he or she is. Principles and standards of a spiritually tilted society have enormous value to the individual who seeks to live meaningfully, purposefully each day.

What have I said? You enjoy connectedness and

You Have Relatedness—You Are in Relation To!

4. Put truth on your side.

Truth does not always come in soft gloves, but always with hope and purpose. Even if it hurts in the short run, truth never fails to be helpful and healthful over the long haul. Some of these statistics came out of research several years ago, but they are still instructive.[15]

- Drug use and intoxication are more prevalent during homosexual encounters than heterosexual activities.
- A gay lifestyle is less healthy than a heterosexual lifestyle.

- In some surveys, three out of four psychiatrists claim that, on average, gays are not as happy as non-gays.
- Up to 70 percent of active gays suffer from some sexually transmitted disease.
- A bigger percentage of practicing gays are alcohol dependent than non-gays.
- A larger percentage of active gays are unhappier and less fulfilled than non-gays.
- On average, lifespan of gays is 60 percent shorter than non-gays—less than 15 percent live past age 65.

Even if the numbers were slightly skewed, the preponderance of findings should not tax the credibility of an honest, inquiring life. One thing is sure—

Truth Is a Dependable Friend!

5. Welcome tradition, principles and the Scriptures.

Think of tradition as helpful beliefs and customs handed to you by those who were before you. However, there is confusion over tradition and traditionalism. Someone I appreciated very much explained the difference like this: Tradition is living (values) of dead people and traditionalism is dead (values) of living people . . . tradition is a source of life and traditionalism is the occasion of its death.

Tradition, then, is the best values from the past working now to help us to overcome mistakes, to correct errors, and to open doors to a grander experience of life. Does a gay lifestyle square with tradition?

"Are you kidding!" one of my three friends replied. "Tradition is my adversary!"

Principles represent codes of thinking and behavior that are close buddies of tradition. When the boss asked an accountant interviewing for a job, "How much is 2 + 2?" the numbers cruncher replied, "How much do you want it to be?"

Was he acting on principle? Obviously not.

Principles lift the way a person thinks and cleans up the way he lives. Consider them as collective, reliable guidelines that worked for others before you, will work for you today, and will contribute to your completeness now. Those principles will be around long after you and I are gone.

Add the scriptures which are sacred writings—and more. They are the Hope Manifesto—and more. Salvation's Bill of Rights—and more. A Charter for Recovery—and more. Wisdom of the Ages—and more. The Blueprint To Wholeness—and more. A lighthouse in the darkness—and more. An anchor in stormy seas—and more. A sinner's lifeline—and more. A demon's worst nightmare—and more. A successful person's manual—and more. The scriptures are all of these—and more.

I see the scriptures as the mind and thoughts of God spoken through people, to people, in such a way that they can be used as resource for insight and direction in daily life. This is not to anyone's detriment, but to everyone's wholeness.

"I don't look at it that way," a gay friend said. "People, conditions, perceptions, and understanding have gone through eons of change since the Bible was written. Some of what may have been true then isn't necessarily true now."

But the truth is that anyone who applies the scriptures to behavior— this includes sexual behavior—doesn't lose anything worth having. *Alert: Disregard the scriptures at your own peril!*

Tradition, Principles and Scripture— at Your Service!

6. Approve your beginnings.

On the surface, my three friends wouldn't question who gave them life, but behind closed doors, their lifestyle occasionally caused them doubts. One explained, "Some people are gay, some are straight, yet, I'm called on to believe that all originated equally with the same God. If my lifestyle is wrong and unless God discriminates, why should I think I am a product of divine intelligence?"

What do I mean when I say "beginnings"?

- Every person is a deliberate act of God; no other explanation fully accounts for the intricacies of life.
- Our "selfhood"—the essential qualities of being a person—is from God. It is not a quirk of nature with some internal wiring misconnected or disconnected. As a deliberate act of God, selfhood has purpose: life. This is not only breath, but the ultimate meaning you find by fulfilling your purpose for being given breath.

God Did Away with Discrimination Long Before Each Person Was Born. From Your Beginnings, You Were Blessed with Birth Rights!

7. Reassert birthright.

Regardless of sexual preference, we have much in common with all other people. For example, no one has a say about being born and to whom. No one is given a choice about the color of his skin, or whether he is born to wealth or poverty, or in what nation and culture.

We also share our "being"—that wondrous, superb essence that uniquely identifies each one as a person. Being comes with certain inalienable qualities and opportunities from birth.

The Ability to Choose Is a Birthright!

One of the most thrilling and irrevocable qualities of being is the right to make choices about the way we think, act, and live. In spite of being unsighted, my friend, Ginny Owens, could choose to develop a full life which led to becoming a popular recording artist of sacred music—and she did.

No other life form possesses a right like that. For example, I watched a mother grizzly on Alaska's Kodiak Island swing into action when faced with a threat to her cubs. She attacked a male much bigger than she and sent him running away in humiliating retreat. The act was prompted by instinct, not willful choice.

The ability to make choices can be neutralized, sidelined, polluted, corrupted, nullified, and manipulated, but it cannot and will not be cancelled.

In my view, sexual preference may involve a number of factors, but acting on that preference (behavior) is determined by choices. Heredity, environment, circumstances, or any other factors before and after birth may be influential and may denote a predisposition to homosexuality, however, these factors are not on the front lines.

Researchers at Northwestern University concluded that "genetic, hormonal factors may contribute to sexual orientation, but do not determine it."[16] Another researcher added that there could be a "predisposition to homosexuality." If there is, to act out homosexuality is a choice.[17]

The ability to make choices is power to determine the direction for life *and* its contents, regardless of external or internal forces. A person may choose his contacts, environment, associations, relationships, the way he lives or fails to live, and which people he will allow into his life. There may be obstacles, but still that right is his turf.

What about my three friends?

Two chose to leave the lifestyle of their past. Both were already confessing believers. Each one told me this journey to healing included a rediscovery of the amazing power of grace and faith and a fuller understanding of the purpose for his life. One described his new understanding by saying, "My purpose is not primarily self-gratification. Not even personal fulfillment. It is to honor God."

To honor God.

That caught my attention in a heartbeat and has stuck with me.

It has also caused me to think further. Self-gratification and personal fulfillment, meaning and enjoyment are all God-given and are most authentic when they grow from a life lived "to honor God."

Both of these friends are the caliber of people you would be blessed to know.

The third friend made several starts in another direction, but didn't last.

"I can't," he said. "I can't!"

I responded, "Progress involves process. 'We' is at the heart of process. 'We' consists of You, God, qualified professional counselors, and contributing others. The difference between *can't* and *can* is apostrophe *t* and *we*."

When you can't, *we* can.

You have it on good authority—God's!

Twelve Ways to Respond to a Gay Family Member or Friend without Compromising Convictions, Forsaking Faith, Surrendering Sanity and Giving Up Goodwill

With increasing numbers of people in high places—politicians, ministers, educators, and religious leaders—announcing that they are practicing homosexuals, loved ones, friends, people in the pew, and neighbors are mystified. They are also looking for ways to deal with them.

"What can we do?"

"What should we do?"

"When can we do it?"

1. Learn, not squirm.

Ignorance is an effective way to lose friends and turn people off. Ignorance should cause anyone to squirm because there is no excuse for it. So arm yourself with knowledge. It's power! Read about the subject. A wealth of material is available on the Internet, however, I urge you to *beware* of hotheads whether they are pro or con. Often, their information, arguments, and statistics are grossly distorted in favor of their position.

2. Make sense, not offense.

Attitude is radically important. So is treatment of the person. To make sense without being offensive, use the Jesus Rule: What would He say and do? How would He treat the person and issue? This is love with integrity producing thoughts, talk, and actions that reflect what Jesus taught and did. This doesn't require anyone to abandon his faith, traditions, principles, lifestyle, or hopes!

3. Woo, not boo.

Both those who express strong objections to homosexuality and those who champion gay causes drag each other into heated verbal confrontation, sometimes exploding into shouting matches—or worse. Some try to scare gays into submission. Information on this topic can be scary, I agree, but the challenge is to *win winsomely*. Furthermore, it is probably the only method that will actually make a difference.

4. Cheer, not smear.

Be supportive of wholesome characteristics seen in others. Congratulate people for positive aspects of their lives. Encourage them for the good they do, no matter how insignificant it may be.

5. Hug, not slug.

If a person has strong convictions about a homosexual lifestyle, of course he can rant and rave with the scriptures in hand. Save the tirade and spare the loved one or friend—and yourself—the conflict it will generate. But remember, words and acts that hold hands with love don't add up to the approval or acceptance of gay behavior.

6. Tug, not mug.

When an opportunity presents itself to talk with the loved one or friend about matters related to the lifestyle, don't press it. Stay composed. Be gentle, decent, and firm.

7. Embrace, not disgrace.

Do not, I repeat, *do not* attack the essence of the person. "I believe you're wrong and here are the reasons I believe it" is a far cry from saying, "I know you're a dirty person and I'll show why" while thinking under your breath, *You pervert.*

8. Include, not exclude.

Remember, the person is still a family member or a friend. Straight family members should keep that door swinging inward; the results can be positive. I know a son in a gay lifestyle who was the one family member to help his father the most during a terminal illness.

9. Pray, not slay.

Prayer for the loved one or friend (yourself, too) is better than wringing your hands raw in despair, anger, and disgust. Always keep in mind that prayer is an effective method to bring about changes in people and conditions.

10. Chug, not scrub.

Like the old time steam train that chugged along, keep at it. Keep thinking, talking, acting, and praying in ways that demonstrate the Jesus Rule. Good things may come about for the loved one or friend and everyone concerned. Besides, it will be good for everyone. What is the alternative? Resignation to gloom and doom. Those are pig pens. Refuse to wallow in them.

11. Serve, don't swerve.

After a speaking engagement, I was on the way to the airport when a big chunk of rock broke off from an embankment and tumbled directly into my path. Naturally, I swerved to avoid it. That was the right thing to do.

Except for die-hards on each side, the tendency may be to swerve from issues like homosexuality. That's the wrong thing to do. Especially in these days, issues like the ones discussed in this book deserve to be considered intelligently, thoughtfully, faithfully, and openly in families, small groups, classes, sermons, the media, and other public forums.

A pastor told me that he had devoted a series to difficult subjects including homosexuality. When the idea first surfaced, he was apprehensive about its appropriateness. He asked, "Would a discussion on homosexuality be suitable in public, especially a worship environment?"

He wasn't alone. Some other staff members and lay movers and shakers in the congregation voiced the same concerns, but they assured him that he would have their support if he undertook the project. He devoted ten Sunday mornings to the series. The church hadn't witnessed such interest in a very long time. On average, attendance jumped close to 50 percent.

Serve by becoming a catalyst, energizer, and facilitator. Encourage involvement in the church, community, and among friends. And, for goodness sake, take the high road!

Remember, intelligent, thoughtful, and faith-centered treatment of the subject is a winner.

12. Be Humble, not heady.

You can declare, "I believe homosexual behavior is wrong." But so is any thought, word, or deed that is an affront to God, even when attempts are made to soften the blow.

A friend sent me a cartoon by e-mail. A delegation of church members are in the pastor's office to deliver a petition requesting the minister stop using the word *sinner* and instead, use the phrase "morally challenged."

Descriptions and words change nothing.

Don't misunderstand me: I don't believe that profanity from a person's lips is equal to a gay lifestyle. However, both remind us that everyone is a sinner and in need of mercy from the Lord. Sins may vary from person to person, but human need doesn't. The impact and severity differ, but not the essence. Every wrong is wrong. A sin is a sin is a sin.

Martin Luther, father of the Protestant Reformation, described it in these words: "The ultimate proof of the sinner is that he does not recognize his own sin."[18]

In all dealings with a person who is gay, be humble not heady and certainly not hypocritical. Remind yourself, "I, too, am a sinner."

A. P. S.
(Author's Postscript)

The percentage of population in America who are into a gay lifestyle may be as low as 0.5 percent. Some claim up to 10 percent. Heat surrounding the subject seems to get hotter by the day. Interest groups scramble to adopt strategies and intensify campaigns to legitimize the gay lifestyle in families, society, and churches.

Some church groups caught up in the struggle are battered with claims that it is a matter of civil rights. "Not so fast," opponents reply, "It's a scriptural issue." They ask, "What does the Bible say?"

Many on all sides agree that it is a moral issue. Some question, "Can gays be Christians?"

"Of course," the others answer.

Should they be elected leaders in churches? "Absolutely not!" responds one group.

"That's ludicrous!" shouts the other. "They are products of further enlightenment. God didn't stop speaking with the last book in the Bible."

"Should they serve as ministers?"

"That's a no-brainer," claims one side. "Not unless they choose to renounce homosexual behavior."

"Wrong! Very wrong!" replies the other. "They are God's children, too. And they have so much to offer the church and society."

And the debate goes on.

Some say that sexual preference is caused by environmental, cognitive, and biological factors, genetics and inborn hormonal influences over which a person has no input or control. It's nature vs. nurture warfare. On the other hand, suppose that genetic and hormonal factors do contribute to sexual preference. Do they *determine* it? One body of research answers, "No."[19] There is another finding I see as compelling and hopeful. Remember the research I have already mentioned: Even if sexual preference is not a choice, to act on it is a choice.

When all the smoke is blown away, the power to choose remains unblemished. I am reminded of Joshua when he challenged the waffling Hebrews, ". . . choose for yourselves this day" (Josh. 24:14, NIV). Without power to choose, there is power for nothing.

It changes everything.

Discussion Room

Agree	Disagree	
☐	☐	It takes all kinds of people to make the world go 'round.
☐	☐	Since I don't like gays, I don't have to love them.
☐	☐	The fifth person—Holier Than Thee—is as sinful as a practicing homosexual.
☐	☐	The bedroom is strictly and exclusively personal—what's done there is no one's business except the ones in there.
☐	☐	If homosexual preference is caused by environmental and biological factors, heterosexual preference is too.
☐	☐	I wouldn't be upset if a leader in my church were gay.
☐	☐	God brings judgment on gays.
☐	☐	As far as the Bible is concerned, I think God is still revealing His truth.
☐	☐	There is more to life than choices we make.
☐	☐	It's better to live and let live.
☐	☐	If I tolerate homosexuality, I endorse it.
☐	☐	A person can change some things about his life, but not others.
☐	☐	I'm not responsible for the lifestyle of a family member or friend. If one were gay, it wouldn't embarrass me in the least.

Agree	Disagree	
☐	☐	I feel there is so much good in the worst of us, and so much bad in the best of us, that it ill behooves any of us, to find fault with the rest of us.[20]
☐	☐	God loves a person no matter who he is or what he does.

You Might Like to Know

- According to a prominent counselor, four environmental causes of homosexual behavior in adults could include homosexual experiences in childhood, an abnormal family setting (for example, an absentee father), unusual sexual experiences (including exposure to pornography early in life and molestation while a child) and cultural influences (including acceptance of homosexuality as a preferred way of life or classroom instruction which teaches the lifestyle is normal and OK).[21]
- Over a fifteen-year period, counseling for more than 400 gay men included reparative therapy. A third of them experienced no change in behavior. Another one-third experienced "significant improvement," and the rest experienced "cure" and changed their lifestyle.[22]
- The estimate that 10 percent of the population in America is gay is based on information by Dr. Alfred Kinsey in 1948. In their book *Kinsey, Sex, and Fraud*, Edward Eichel and Dr. Judith Reisman insist that the Kinsey numbers are overstated due to the subjects who were used to come to *his* conclusion.[23] Updated research suggests the number is from 1 to 3 percent.
- In reply to the argument that sexual preference is a matter of civil rights—a term usually reserved for a disadvantaged group that society has oppressed—some claim that gays are far from being disadvantaged and that the issue is moral and social rather than civil. Some champions of Native American,

African American and Hispanic causes insist that the focus on the idea of civil rights for the gay lifestyle is at the expense of their causes.

- Recent data indicates there are twenty-three states, the District of Columbia, and more than 180 cities with laws prohibiting selectiveness for employment based on sexual behavior in public and private jobs in the public workplace.[24]
- Results of a particular research indicates that the average household income for gays is up to double the national average. College graduates among gays is three times the national average, and the number of gays in professional and managements positions is also three times the national average.[25] Gay interest groups dispute the income comparison claiming that gays earn up to 40 percent less than heterosexual counterparts.
- If the homosexual community makes up 1 to 3 percent of the population in America (or even 10 percent as some claim), some contend that they are given an unfair degree of political influence.

Prayer for People Whose Sexual Preference Is Different from Mine— and Those That Are the Same

Strong God, it is thrilling to be assured that no one is ever beyond the reach of Your love, outside the limits of Your mercies, removed from the availability of Your strength, over the edge of hope, or past the possibility of new directions in life.

Help those who question and struggle with their sexuality to believe this.

Come to the ones whose sexual behavior is different from mine with new courage to re-examine their inner self directly and honestly.

Renew their confidence that urges can be controlled, adjustments in their best interests can be made, and empowerment to live out the purpose You have for them is as close as You are.

Bless them with joy in living, serenity of soul, and genuine peace with themselves. May they allow You to be the God who brings them into the dimension of life You have in mind.

Help me, welcoming Lord, and others like me, to live in love for those whose preferences are different from mine, to be considerate of their feelings, to learn from them, and to serve as useful influences in their lives.

Save us from flaky smugness, gaudy self-righteousness, superficial arrogance, rabid condemnation, and thoughtless application of personal convictions, remembering that we are also sinners to whom You bring the miracle of grace. In the name of Him who was never ashamed to love people like each of us. Amen.

Good News

God chose you before the world was and brought you into life to be His child . . . Take a closer look at your ways and examine them; lift your heart and hands to God who has chosen you (Eph. 1:4; Lam. 3:40–41).

Chapter Four

"It will help us to be happier."
A clever claim—is it fact or fiction?

Ted and Sally, Live-In Arrangement—No, They Weren't Married!

Growing up, Ted and Sally were delightful children blessed with upstanding middle class families.

In their teens, they had lots of friends and were fairly good students. Sally was exceptional and fun to be around. Ted went to church with his parents, sometimes willingly, sometimes not, but never belligerently.

As for Sally, she demonstrated a lively faith. Church activities and community programs were a core part of her life. She fondly remembered the mission trips when she helped build a health clinic in Mexico and conduct enrichment services for Native American children.

Fresh out of college, Ted and Sally caught each other's eye. They had noticed one another before, but this time was different. Romance was in the air. Ted was no gushy Don Juan, but I'm sure that these lines from *The Beggar's Opera* met with his approval:

> If the heart of a man is depress'd with cares,
> The mist is dispell'd when a woman appears.[26]

If anyone had mentioned that God made man and woman to share love, be full of joy found in a devoted relationship, and experience the satisfaction that comes through commitment to one another in marriage, he wouldn't have heard a single argument from either of them—particularly Sally. However, if anyone had thought that Ted and Sally would never live as if they were married before marriage, he would have been wrong—and very surprised. A popular word for this arrangement is *cohabitation.*

By definition, cohabitation is two unmarried people of the opposite sex living as if they are married—two roommates who are romantic partners, sharing a common living space without a public commitment such as a wedding.

In recent years, cohabitation has skyrocketed by more than 1300 percent and it is rising at a spectacular pace. Furthermore, people of faith have been part of the rise. According to some data, most high school seniors feel it is a good idea to live together before tying the knot. Not to be left out completely, cohabitation has swelled by 50 percent among older persons.

Noting the trend and referring to western nations, Andrew Cherlin of John Hopkins University stated, "Never before in history has it been acceptable for unmarried couples to live together."[27] I've observed some interesting explanations that I feel are factors behind the explosion.

Ten Clever Claims—Fact or Fiction?

1. "It will help us get to know—really know—one another before taking the big leap." I have known couples which found that it opened a Pandora's box of questions about oneself and the partner, developed suspicions, and spread enough distrust to destabilize and eventually destroy any hopes of a relationship.

2. "It will reduce the chances of a divorce." According to research, cohabitation actually increases the risk as much as a whopping 85 percent.[28] Some other reliable data shows that cohabitants have an 80 percent chance of ending their relationship within ten years of beginning the arrangement.[29]

3. "In case things don't work, we'll avoid the shock and cost of a divorce." If the relationship is more than physical, the shared feelings are secure enough and deep enough to pave the way for marriage, a break-up, according to some couples who have gone through it, is tantamount to an emotional tsunami. As far as expense avoidance, maybe not. A person could still be on the hook—and probably should be.

4. "It will help us to better get in touch with our real selves." That depends on which real self the person is talking about. Apparently, a self other than the one that has the right to prosper. Within each person is a sin-tilted self. The prophet admitted it when he confessed, "I am undone and a person with sinful lips" (Isa. 6:5). That self needs no encouragement. It does very well on its own. The self that longs for spiritual connection and a life on the growing edge is the one that deserves steady recognition.

5. "It will make our marriage stronger." Less than half of cohabitants eventually marry and they are 50 percent more prone than those who do not cohabit to divorce early in marriage.[30] Living together prior to the "I do" is a leading contribution to failure of marriage after the "I do." A young woman who went this route was eager to let me know how much she agreed with the counselor who said, "Cohabitation is an invisible, front-end cancer on marriage."[31]

6. "It is a way for us to be freer with ourselves and one another and to achieve fulfillment." Freedom that is actually freeing and fulfillment that is genuinely fulfilling are not developed by activities that fail to meet the essence of personhood—the "you" God gave you life to become.

7. "It will help us to be happier people." According to the National Institute of Mental Health, cohabitants suffer a higher rate of depression and are more irritable, anxious, worried, and unhappy.[32] With all the negatives that attach themselves to cohabitation, my experiences have proved that more individuals in the arrangement are less happy than married individuals.

8. "It will prepare us for married life." This argument represents a relational ignorance. A person cannot prepare for "what isn't at the moment" (marriage) by doing "what is unreal at the moment" (living as if married). Only real hands-on experience works.

9. "It will be a reliable trial balloon." It is important to remember that marriage is one thing in life that does not come with a trial period. It isn't something a person can buy with a money-back guarantee.

10. "It will prepare us for greater pleasures during intimacy in our marriage." Scientific studies disagree. It is true that cohabitation provides easier access to a partner in sex. But, as pointed out in one body of research, it is bold fiction to think that the arrangement will lead to more satisfaction during intimacy after married. "If a couple abstains from sex before marriage, they are more likely than those who cohabit to enjoy sex afterwards. Sexual satisfaction rises considerably after marriage."[33]

Guidebook Answers—
Seven Step Emancipation Plan

First Step: Conduct the comparison test

For the test, select as many as five couples who are or have been cohabitants and objectively evaluate them. As a result of cohabitation:

- Are/Were they happier, more adjusted, and more complete than successful married couples you know?
- Are they enjoying/Did they enjoy a greater degree of satisfaction with themselves and life?
- Are/Were they more productive persons?
- Are/Were they more congenial with family members?
- Is/Was stability and growth their longer term objective?
- Are/Were they more spiritual than before moving in together?

- Would others become stronger and better people by emulating them?

The effectiveness and reliability of the Comparison Test is completely dependent upon honesty.

Second Step: Back the future into the now

It starts with questions like: "Ten years from today, would I want to be a cohabitant?"

"Fifteen years?"

"When I have children?" "Grandchildren?"

"When I die?"

If it would not be an acceptable arrangement at any of those times, why is the arrangement acceptable today?

If the answer is "No" to any these questions, the answer should be "No" in the present as well. If anyone doesn't want to be in cohabitation later in life, he/she can successfully repel arguments trying to convince him/her to live in it sooner? Think long term.

Third Step: Participate in the personal desirability quiz

Consider this question head on: "Does cohabitation contribute to becoming the caliber of person someone should or would want to have as a life partner?" During the next seven days, invest thirty minutes a day in the answer. Take a sheet of paper. Write *yes* at the top on the left half and *no* at the top right half. Under each one, list every reason that comes to mind. Afterwards, review these lists once a day for four weeks. Jot down additional reasons when you think of them.

ADVISORY: FOOL, JIGGLE, TWIST, SIDESTEP OR WHITEWASH THE TRUTH AND YOU LOSE!

Fourth Step: Introduce the divine formulation equation

Here is the way it's done.

"Was I made for an arrangement like this?"

"Would this lifestyle, even when temporary, reflect the purpose behind my life?"

"What about the gift of life to me?"

"The reason of life for me?"

"The direction of life for me?"

An irrevocable truth each one can take to the bank is

God Created Everyone for
the High Road in Life—*Everyone!*

If you have entered into this kind of pseudo-marriage relationship, the nagging little voice inside may have already made the answer loud and clear, but other noises have been allowed to distort it.

Fifth Step: Exercise the right of refusal

There is a two-sided Rule of Life that applies to behavior. The first side is based on the premise that every person has a golden opportunity to decline to act in a certain way before the act is begun. Here's the Rule:

WITH HELP, A PERSON NEVER HAS
TO STOP ANYTHING HE DOESN'T START.

The second side is based on the premise that once begun, a person can choose to change directions. The Rule of Life is:

WITH HELP, ANYONE WHO STARTS
SOMETHING HE SHOULDN'T HAVE STARTED
CAN CORRECT HIS COURSE OF ACTION.

Jesus had these rules in mind when He said, "I have come that you may have life and have it abundantly . . . in all of its fullness, wholeness, completeness, splendor" (John 10:6). Combine his statement with the words of Paul, a devoted believer, who personally experienced this, and you will lose every shred of doubt. "By His power at work in us, God is able to do far more abundantly than all we ask or think" (Eph. 3:20).

Talk over the advantages of stopping or changing what you may at times wish you had not started. Maintain a calm and collected setting with an open mind, receptive heart, and willing life. A mutual agreement is possible.

Sixth Step: Start on a make-it-right course

Be sure to involve your partner when possible.
What are some of the choices available?

- Separation—A new beginning in which each goes his/her own way. If the arrangement were little more than a convenient sexual relationship and mostly thought of as a temporary rendezvous, separation should be at the top of the list. In cohabitation, a person is most likely headed toward it anyway. (However, if there is already a family and or a serious commitment to each other and there is a loving relationship, separation is probably not a sensible option.)
- Suspension—If there are serious plans of marriage, put a hold on living like a married couple and decide on a morally, emotionally, and socially enhancing alternative which agrees with spiritual values.
- Marriage—Maybe the ceremony could be immediate, but make sure there is a firm commitment to each other. In my own experience, several couples chose this option (one couple was already grandparents!). After review, prayer, dedication, and commitment with agreements, I have been honored to perform ceremonies, rejoice with them at the birth of children, and share the joy of welcoming grandchildren into the world.

Seventh Step: Take at least one step today to resolve the problem

Follow-up with another step.
And another.
And another.

Take each step with confidence that a wrong turn can be corrected because . . .

The Power a Mistake Manifests in a Person's Daily Life Is in Direct Proportion to the Power the Person Allows the Mistake to Manifest!

By activating the greater strength that is available, the power of a wrong can be split and reduced to the point that it is powerless. Have no doubt: Whatever needs to be done can be done. If something *should* be done, it *could* be done. Anyone who is partner to the need can be partner to the answer. In hand is the capacity to be a doer—*the* doer, if necessary.

Triumph is on the side of doers.

What final decision did Ted and Sally make?

Marriage.

After a year of live-in arrangement, they realized there was more to life than continuing on the other side of right. Both were also re-awakened spiritually. "The truth is we had to send spiritual and family values on vacation when we moved in together," they both said.

I was thrilled to perform the ceremony, and to witness firsthand their personal and family development. If God's response to the outcome for Ted and Sally could have been heard, I would not at all be surprised if the Lord led a cheer that raised the roof.

I know I felt like doing it!

A. P. S.
(Author's Postscript)

When asked what is behind the meteoric rise in cohabitation, from my experience, one cause is a weakening moral climate. Attacks from many directions—in and out of churches—have been like waves on a Florida beach, one after the other. They have led to a redrawing of boundaries for right and wrong. In response, standards have been watered down or reasoned away. In these conditions, people, including believers, become easier pickings for fictitious claims like the ones I mentioned.

Cohabitation represents a seismic shift in culture; living together is being substituted for traditional romance and courtship. Dr. Barbara Dafoe Whitehead, the distinguished sociologist at Rutgers University, refers to these times as "cultural cluelessness." She explained that "most societies have had a script and young adults have been guided through that script. Now the script (has been) radically revised (and) nobody knows what it is anymore or people have torn it up."[34]

But cohabitation for people in the retirement crowd has other dimensions. Some reasons for opting out of marriage include tax advantages, loss of pension benefits, the ability to share expenses, insurance, protection of assets, and Social Security provisions. Most of these people believe in marriage and, at one time, were married. They are faced head-on by disapproving children, even grandchildren. Whatever the reasons for cohabitation, they have a full challenge on their hands trying to square it with their faith and values—at least, that's what some have told me. Others have skipped cohabitation because of their long-held values and faith.

I remember Harry and Diana whose spouses died when they were in their sixties. In retirement years, a marvelous thing happened—the love bug knocked on their door. They wanted to be with each other, and, due to limited financial resources, a live-in arrangement would have been very advantageous.

"There are some things money can't and won't buy," they said before the wedding ceremony. "Our faith, integrity, and reputation are among them."

Discussion Room

Agree	Disagree	
☐	☐	It's a new day. New ways are okay.
☐	☐	I know married believers who would be better off if they were single.
☐	☐	Don't get in a stew. If cohabitation is really wrong, God will forgive.

Agree	Disagree	
☐	☐	I know unmarried people living together, and they're happy.
☐	☐	Cohabitation is no worse than others wrongs.
☐	☐	With the social environment the way it is, sex education at younger ages and physical development in earlier years, it's unrealistic to believe everyone ought to resist cohabitation.
☐	☐	Lack of guidance and instruction in the home is the reason for moral decay.
☐	☐	Public education should reinforce strong values based on Judeo-Christian principles.
☐	☐	Christians should be more open minded
☐	☐	I'd rather be a cohabitant than a sex offender.
☐	☐	Faith-based instruction should be included in public schools
☐	☐	It's my body. I can do what I want with it.
☐	☐	My church is offensive in its approach and teachings about matters like cohabitation.
☐	☐	If one of my parents or grandparents passed away and the surviving spouse entered a live-in arrangement, I would be very angry.
☐	☐	Something that may be wrong for one person may not be wrong for another. Something that may be right for one isn't necessarily right for everyone
☐	☐	If I had it to do over, I would consider a live-in arrangement before getting married.

Agree	Disagree	
☐	☐	Weak religious faith and participation contributes to higher rates of cohabitation and lower rates of marriage to the person with whom one cohabits.
☐	☐	If a person is really a believer, he or she will marry before living with the fiancé or friend.
☐	☐	Cool it! In time, the attitude of the younger generation will change. Their behavior will more closely align with values of their parents and grandparents.
☐	☐	God will provide the strength for a person to do the right thing.
☐	☐	The way God wants a person to live is the most enjoyable, satisfying, gratifying, successful option available.

The Word on the Street

First Question:

If you could go back, would you live with your wife or husband before you married? Why or why not?

Responses:

No . . . My parents would have disowned me.

Not on my life! . . . My siblings would have "killed" me (made her miserable).

No, but not because of me . . . My fiancé wouldn't agree. She proved to be right.

No, but I would have if I could have . . . My fiancé was several months pregnant when we found out. We married immediately.

No . . . It would have embarrassed a lot of what my family and I have stood for.

No . . . Both of us believed that marriage is a sacred responsibility.

No . . . I believed that something wrong will not ever turn out right. Still do.

No . . . We did and lived to regret it (the couple divorced. Some reasons were attributed to developments as a result of cohabitation).

Yes . . . It's not as bad as some religious people want to make it.

Yes . . . We wouldn't have been hypocrites (about active sex life).

Yes . . . Well, I think so. It would have given us a head start on realities that have come up in our marriage.

The results were, 72 percent indicated no—28 percent, yes. More than 60 percent of the men would not have cohabited whereas 80 percent of the women felt the same way.

Second Question:

What was one lesson you learned from a son, daughter or grandchild who experienced a live-in arrangement?

Responses:

I couldn't do anything about it.

All of our complaining plus "righteous pontificating" equaled nothing.

I could love him anyway.

Never cut a family member off (from the family).

I could be firm without being obnoxious.

It's okay to show that negative behavior hurts us (parents).

We (parents) allowed ourselves to be intimidated and it didn't help. We became doormats.

Prayers mean something even when it seems they are disappearing into a black hole.

Firmness and honesty are influential.

Don't be bashful. Speak up, but in a calm, collected, reasoned, positive spirit.

(Cohabitation) wasn't anything twenty-five years didn't cure (in mid-life, the son returned to the values of his parents).

Don't give up on a child.

I can cope with disappointment.

I must live my life, not my grandchild's.
Depend on God no matter what happens.

Prayer for Value-based Behavior

In Your mercy, Lord, stir us to consider cohabitation with open hearts and minds. Deepen the desire to strive for fullest realization of personal potential and live above the norm set by environment and society. Grant reassurance that lasting emotional and mental wholeness depends on living according to Your plan.

Grant freedom from fear of public commitment and strengthen with courage to admit that honesty, integrity, truth, and other life-enhancing values remain the same from one generation to the next.

Gracious God, dispatch the willingness necessary to put excuses aside. Bring the humility needed to depend on You for the power to make changes which agree with the divine purpose for having life. Through the One who opens doors to everything anyone could ever need. Amen.

Good News

God has a great investment in you so do not allow anyone or anything to enslave you . . . I say to the Lord, "I have nothing good apart from you" (1 Cor. 7:23; Ps. 16:2).

57

Chapter Five

Single and expecting a child—
"How could I let this happen to me!"

Marcia—Unplanned (Maybe Unwanted) Pregnancy

In this country, nearly half of the births are to unwed mothers—many more than half of all births in one state during a recent year. According to the Secretary of Health for that state, "As far as I know, there is nothing on the horizon that will change this (phenomenon) in the foreseeable future."[35]

Dr. Gary L. Rose of the Medical Institute for Sexual Health, added, "Like casual drug use in the '60s, America's current culture has accepted casual, 'protected' sex as the norm. There is a critical need for behavior modification—risk avoidance, not mere risk reduction—if the trend is to reverse."[36]

The drastic spike in births to unmarried women is having an enormous social, emotional, relational, and spiritual impact on families and communities. Not long ago, I knew six young women who were pregnant at the same time—five were never married.

Like these women, Marcia had personality plus, was attractive, blessed with a good family, favored by advantages, active in church—or was—and had not lived an environmentally driven lifestyle. She was also a standout at school, in the community, and among her peers.

Did Marcia agree that human life is wonderfully made?

Absolutely!

She was convinced that the incredibly intricate combinations leading to a person with body, mind, and spirit showed the meticulous involvement of a divine hand. Nevertheless, she was pregnant. And she harbored questions about the birth.

Would the baby be fully welcomed?

Could she handle the child at this time in her life?

The one that especially got under her skin was, "How could I let this happen?"

Then there were questions about the father. Did she want to marry him? Was he someone she wanted to share her life with? Would he shoulder responsibilities for bringing another life into the world?

She felt stymied and had already begun to consider the options faced by single expectant mothers:

a. Abortion
b. Give birth and keep the child.
c. Give birth and offer the child for adoption.

The option to give birth and keep the child would shift her responsibilities, juggle financial demands, and require changes in use of time. It could also influence her goals, dreams, friendships, relationships, choices of activities, her menu, habits, attitude about herself, and her thinking about others and life.

It seemed that abortion would solve many issues. However, it would raise another one more imposing than the proverbial 800-pound gorilla: Was it the right thing to do?

If I gave birth and offered the child for adoption, what would that say about me? she thought. *I have my right to the child. This baby is my flesh and blood.*

If the birth were considered an unwelcomed intruder, there could be a long line of "what ifs" and "I sure wish I had _____." Marcia was clear headed enough to realize that at the moment, "what ifs" and "I sure wish I had _____" would not alter facts and that none of these facts had any problem-solving grace, not even a smidgen.

Seven Guidebook Answers—It's About Life

1. Level with life.

One of our most common faults is the tendency to be dishonest about uncertain situations and unpleasant challenges. And it is a fault that has some of the most impoverishing consequences.

A pregnancy presents unique challenges. Just ask any mother. One made it very clear when she said, "I didn't dream there would be so many new demands on my life."

Becoming a single parent often injects fear into the equation. But by the time of birth, any euphoria may be swallowed by uneasiness, doubts, and a generous dose of fear.

Life does not grow on dishonesty. We need square thinking with what is real.

If you are expecting a child, say, "Yes, I'm pregnant"—the body already knows this, but what about the emotional and mental aspects?

Comedian Phyllis Diller said, "The strongest craving of a pregnant woman is *not* to be pregnant." You may wish you weren't pregnant. If so say, "Yes, I wish I weren't pregnant."

You may not want the child. Then say, "No, I don't want the child."

Your family may not want you to have the child. Then admit that, "My family doesn't want me to have the child."

Friends may bombard you with well-intentioned, yet confusing ideas about what you should do. And you would just as soon they stuff it. If so, "I wish they'd shut up." (It might not be a bad idea to ask them to give the subject a rest.)

You may wonder how on earth you can make it with a child. Admit to yourself that, "I don't have the foggiest idea how I can handle this pregnancy and the responsibilities of having the child."

You may be beating yourself up for getting pregnant. Go ahead and say, "I blew it, really blew it!"

Do you get the idea about what I mean when I say, level with life?

FRANKNESS = HEALING POWER IN YOUR HANDS!

2. Lift two lives at once.

Before long, the question front and center becomes, "What am I to do now?"

Is ending the pregnancy a viable option? Is it the *best* option? What about keeping the child—is that the *best* option? Or giving birth and then putting the child up for adoption—is that the *best* course of action?

The operative word obviously is best, but for whom—the child? Mother? Family? Everyone else involved?

A grand epiphany moment happens when you ask, "Is everything now all about me?

Is even a simple majority of everything about me? Is it overwhelmingly, or should it be overwhelmingly, about the life which is inside of me? If it is about the life within me, am I zeroed out? Where do I come into the picture? Or, do I?"

I remember the shocked look on faces when I stated the following: "When unmarried people consent to sexual behavior where pregnancy is possible, both of them surrender the claim to priority consideration in what follows." Priority then becomes what is best for the unborn child. (Where does that place the expectant mother? I'll get to it in a moment.)

- Abortion—best for the unborn?
- Keeping the child—best for the unborn?
- Making the child a gift to a full family through adoption—best for the unborn?

An old rule of baseball states two players cannot occupy first base at the same time. That principle may be true in baseball, but not in pregnancy and the art of living.

First Principle

In the Sermon on The Mount, Jesus dared to convey a remarkable truth at work in the spiritual world and life when He said, "Seek first the kingdom of God and what is right. Then whatever else is needed will be provided" (Matt. 6:33). When that which should be first is first, all else arranges itself into appropriate levels. Likewise, when the lowest priority is treated as if it is first, the top priority is relegated to last place and everything goes out of line.

Jesus further referred to this principle when He told some followers that a person who wants to save his life will lose it and anyone who wants to find his life will save it (Luke 9:24).

In pregnancy, establishing priority for the unborn lifts both the unborn and mother to priority status. That is, what is best for the unborn is—or will prove to be—best for mother, too.

3. Litigate responsibly.

The woman isn't the only one who contributed to the pregnancy. Her partner has obligations, too.

Depending on the decision about the child, consider helping the father and his family see the value of living up to those obligations.

Legal steps may also be necessary. Anyone unable to afford a lawyer may find free counsel in the community. A social service agency like the Salvation Army, United Way, or Catholic Charities might provide information.

On the other hand, maybe you wouldn't dream of sharing your life with the father of your child. You had just as soon forget that he ever existed. In that case, you may want to dismiss him from any further contact or involvement with you. But it would be wise to check out any legal rights he may have and under what conditions he has those rights.

4. Live healthy.

Thoughtful physicians at Columbia University Medical Center, Department of Obstetrics and Gynecology, like to remind people that an expectant mother lives for two people—more, if a multiple birth.

An organization devoted to the well-being of children, BabyFit.com, expresses a potent reality through its motto, "Healthy Babies Start With Healthy Moms."

However, a healthy life is more than one sided. It encompasses a total healthcare program.

The Body

Physical well-being includes:

- Use of recommended vitamin supplements
- Regular exercise several times a week (you'll feel better)
- Weight control will do special wonders for you, too
- A balanced, nutritious diet. Without it, the unborn's growth and development of the brain and immune system could be affected. An improper diet could also be a source of birth defects
- And more, because there's more to life than bread, broccoli, and beans.

Lifestyle

From ancient times, the impact of a person's behavior on his or her health has been recognized. But with the advances in medical, technological, mental, and social sciences, the extent of those effects has become much clearer. For example—decayed teeth, distorted face, and diminished body as a result of meth use.

A well-known physician friend put it bluntly: "A person can't live like hell and enjoy a body and mind fit for heaven!"

Practical steps include:

- Use of tobacco products—out the window
- Alcohol consumption—down the drain
- Pot and other drugs—waste them
- Night out with the girls—not now
- Undisciplined eating—put a lid on it
- Party animal—trash it

- Sleep deprivation—forget it
- Profane, filthy language—a thing of the past
- Constructive, wholesome activities—by all means
- Oversight of health professionals, as much as possible—definitely. They're available and there is an abundance of help from the Internet.

While I'm on it, how about putting a hold on consumption of caffeine? A pregnant person should avoid other sickness enhancing stuff like she would a malignant melanoma.

A Positive Lifestyle Benefits Everyone!

A healthy life is more than a litany of do's and don'ts, check-ups, sonograms, and the expertise of the pros. For instance, consider various associations. Friends form part of one's primary association—people who directly affect the person's life. They are the people you share experiences with in more than a casual way. Someone told me that friends are the people you can depend on to depend on you. I agreed that, to some extent, a person is who and what friends are. But humans are more than blood and bones. They are social creations, therefore, it is reasonable to claim that friends affect a person's health.

But we don't have to go as far as friendships to have relationships that influence our health. Lamenting his son's arrest, a father said, "He was in the wrong place at the wrong time with the wrong people." He wasn't referring to close friends, just to people with whom his son shared the same location for a very brief time. Want an example? You don't have to go any further than second-hand smoke.

FRIENDS AND ASSOCIATIONS ARE IMPORTANT—AND MADE BY CHOICE.

5. Lavish developmental advantages.

Respected researchers claim that a child's behavior may be programmed during pregnancy, stating that "maternal anxiety (during pregnancy) enhances the susceptibility of the child to disorders like attention deficit and hyperactivity disorder." Specialists at the Catholic University of Leuven (Belgium) agree that "non-genetic factors play a role in commonly diagnosed children's disorders" and described them as "prenatal factors on developmental processes of the brain."[37]

On the other hand, positive attention offers a developmental advantage every expectant mother should want for a child. Here are some recommended starters.

- Singing—music with lyrics that have value to them (forget rap, hip-hop, and other songs fit for the garbage dump)
- Words of affection and hopes for the one yet-to-be-born—"I love you" . . . "I believe you'll be an inspiration to others" . . . "God is growing you" . . . "I'm sure you have a wonderful future ahead of you" . . . "You'll do well, I know"
- Soft, gentle strokes across the stomach—they're soothing, assuring, calming, and comforting to the unborn
- Phrases of cheer about the day—"The sunshine is so nice" . . . "The rain is really refreshing, isn't it?" . . . "Isn't it a beautiful day?" . . . "You'd love the color of the flowers today" . . . "We'll make it through this tough spot."

A friend who is a pre-natal authority insists that these pre-birth activities could be helpful to everyone during pregnancy.

6. Leave the lingering loser lullaby where it belongs.

A failure can be incredibly tenacious. Like butter on hot biscuit, it can melt into a person's psyche and fill his soul with doubt and fear until defeat is stacked on defeat. But not if a failure is left where it belongs—in the day before today.

A Mistake Is Not a Morgue!

At least, it doesn't have to be. King of the Israelites and one of the most beloved figures in the Old Testament, David, made a reprehensible mistake when he ordered his leading general into battle where he was marked for certain death so that the king could have the general's beautiful wife. It worked. Ultimately, David owned up to his grievous act (Psalm 51) and lived out life with purpose.

Consider making this your mantra: "Been there and done that, but not again."

7. Lay feelings and perceived needs on God's care.

The Almighty will not leave an expectant mother high and dry to slug it out by herself. God is where she is with help, hope, and healing.

God is now where you are. Tomorrow, God will be where you are before you get there.

(If you intentionally ended a pregnancy, focus on points six and seven to put a yesterday that deserves to forever remain yesterday and to reach toward a future that welcomes you as a special friend.)

What was Marcia's decision?

After considerable struggle and soul searching, she chose adoption because that offered the best prospects for the most complete life for her child, a full family setting in a caring, believing environment from the moment of birth.

In my experience of helping pregnant single women over many years, this decision has usually proven to work out best.

Marcia said that it was necessary to leave "me" behind in coming to the decision. She explained that the child became the most important consideration, not Marcia. She made the choice to think of her act as a gift to the child—the gift of a more complete future from the time of birth and a gift to a family who longed for a child and would love, nurture, and provide more opportunities than she could offer.

"It also proved to be a gift to me," Marcia later claimed.

"With time, I was able to move toward some dreams I had prior to the pregnancy."

She thinks about the boy occasionally, but has overcome every doubt that she made the right decision.

Marcia also knew that she had been forgiven—she had been.

And she believed that a complete family of her own was in her future.

It was!

"God is good," Marcia said, "even when we sometimes aren't."
I can vouch for that!

A. P. S.
(Author's Postscript)

In pregnancy, an expectant mother has exclusive control over the unborn. That makes pregnancy one of the most direct opportunities to exercise leadership and to do something good by doing what is best for someone who is helpless and dependent.

Previously, I indicated that an expectant mother also comes out ahead when the best interest of the child is put first. Those interests serve everyone's short-term and long-term interests. Sometimes, however, it is necessary to walk away from selfish sentimentalism, distorted perception, and unreasonable emotionalism.

Just suppose for a moment that your circumstances and capabilities (or lack of them) make it wise to consider adoption. You may struggle with:

"But it's my flesh and blood."

"Being with the birth mother (me) outweighs the value of adoptive parents."

"I have my rights."

"I'll do it my way."

"I wouldn't think of giving up my baby!"

WHOSE CONSIDERATION SHOULD COME FIRST? WHO LOSES WHEN THE FIRST PRINCIPLE IS PUT IN PLAY?

Just in case you may want to know, there are thousands of believing, married couples who are willing and prepared to provide the full family setting the child deserves. They are also ready to help prior to birth. A reliable local service agency, minister, or physician is a good first step without any obligation.

It may also be sobering to think about this: If an unmarried mother keeps the child, the partner in pregnancy will be visually present in some way throughout her entire life.

Discussion Room

Agree	Disagree	
☐	☐	The younger generation has gone to the dogs.
☐	☐	I would be embarrassed and humiliated if my unmarried child became pregnant.
☐	☐	Public or private schools are no place for sex education.
☐	☐	Morality is strictly a private matter.
☐	☐	I feel uncomfortable considering sexual conduct in a public setting.
☐	☐	An unmarried or never married follower of Christ will not allow himself or herself to be sexually active.
☐	☐	Family is not the place for such delicate subjects as sex education.
☐	☐	My body is also a gift from God.
☐	☐	Parents are too timid or reluctant to discuss sexual matters with children.
☐	☐	Churches have the responsibility to teach youth about sexual issues.
☐	☐	Regardless of instruction in the home, information from the street will have more influence on children.
☐	☐	Sometimes people have to "go with the flow."
☐	☐	The first order of business for a single, pregnant person is to repent.
☐	☐	The male partner in pregnancy is just as responsible as the female.

Agree	Disagree	
☐	☐	Any nincompoop can be a sperm donor. It takes a man to be a father.
☐	☐	God loves an unmarried or never married pregnant woman just as much as He loves anyone at any time in any place.

Once Upon a Time in the Lives of Three Pregnant Women

#1—She had an abortion.

I had to be honest. I didn't want a baby.

I felt I needed a fresh start free of responsibilities for a child.

My family nearly disowned me when I told them I was pregnant.

I am sexually active and still am. Can't help myself.

I thought, *This isn't a good world to bring a baby into.*

I wouldn't want the father as my husband.

I wouldn't want to go through it again.

I'll get over it—I think I will—I hope so.

Yes, I am (a Christian)—at least, I feel that I am.

#2—She gave the child for adoption.

When I made the decision, I was at peace. Then I started second guessing my decision.

After agreeing to adoption, I changed my mind.

I've never been in a struggle like it before returning to my original decision.

Without the support of family, I'm not sure I would have made it.

I renewed my faith.

People at church loved me through what I've gone through.

A judgmental approach wouldn't work with me.

I was surprised at the pool of adoptive couples; there were many possibilities and all were deserving.

I was active in the process that led to the couple that was selected. That helped me, too.

My fiancé and I split.

It has been over two years since the adoption. I think about it, but as times passes, I get better.

From what I know, I'm convinced I made the right decision.

A serious, believing man entered my life. The wedding is coming up. I'm glad God didn't write me off.

#3—She kept the child.

At first, I almost decided in favor of abortion.

Then, I considered keeping the child and followed it with more thinking about advantages of adoption.

Several couples indicated a lot of enthusiasm to adopt the child.

One couple decided not to go ahead with adoption. I wasn't told the reason, but it hurt.

Another didn't meet some requirements by the state; I think the husband may have just passed the age limit.

At that point, I decided against adoption.

Abortion was ruled out. I decided to keep the child.

If I heard it once, I heard it a hundred times—

"Raising a child is a daunting challenge when both parents are involved. What makes you think you can do it by yourself?"

I have been required to be independent in every way possible.

I don't suppose anyone could have fully described what a single parent goes through. I had no idea until the past year or so.

Even with the help of some family members, being a single mother has been no cake walk.

It meant a lot to me to believe that if anyone has done it successfully, I can too.

The father has had no part of my child's life. I feel it's better that way.

I'm active in my church again. It's making a big difference.

I don't believe God got me into this situation, but I have come to believe He is with me to make a life for both of us.

I want to meet the right person for me and marry (at some point).

I've been reminded that to catch fish you have to go where the fish are. I'm making sure I go to the right places.

Prayer for All Mothers

Lord of life, come to those who are expecting a child with new appreciation for what You do to form a human life, with deeper respect for all You have gone through to begin the particular life which is in them, with revived consciousness of the value of a person including themselves, with a sense of life which is more inclusive than themselves, with a vision which sees further than the present moment, with greater ability to think clearly so that they can take into consideration what ought to be, and with a stronger commitment to make right decisions.

Grant to them, loving Heavenly Father, the willingness to listen to others whose insight and experience can be helpful. Draw to their side people who trust in You, who care for them, and are supportive without being demanding and demeaning.

Accepting Lord, may their response to Your amazing love be strong so that pent-up anxieties will be released into Your hands.

Thank You for healing which is available for the emotional and mental disruptions they suffer, the confidence that You can help them come to terms with shortcomings, and the provisions to make their lives more complete. In the name of the One who gives life. Amen.

Good News

Look at what is before your eyes . . . You are a member of God's own family; you belong in the household of the Lord . . . Oh, experience God for yourself and see how gracious He is. See firsthand the abundance of mercies God shares with those who trust in Him (2 Cor. 10:7; Eph. 2:19; Ps. 34:8).

Chapter Six

Quality of life—dismal.
Death—only a matter of time.

Mark, Terminally Ill—Okay to End His Life?

I think of euthanasia as a willful choice to end life. Professionals at the Robert Power Center for Medical Ethics define it as the "intentional killing by act or omission of a human being for his or her alleged benefit."[38]

A physician dubbed the "doctor of death" was convinced that a person has an inalienable right to die. He spent time in prison for helping patients exercise that notion.

Under certain conditions, one state already allows euthanasia while others are thinking about it. In some western nations, it is under consideration.

For anyone with more than an ounce of personal pride, there is no doubt about it: A person's loss of ability to remain self-sufficient and independent can be traumatic. When a person can no longer be involved in enjoyable activities and loses control of bodily and mental functions, it can also be shocking.

When the mind goes, what of value is left?

When suffering overloads good senses, what's a person to do?

The possibility of being a drain on family and friends is abhorrent.

Then, when the likelihood of improvement is only an excursion into la-la land at best and dying is already in motion, should not death by any means be a no-brainer?

Mark, a thirty-something engineer and follower of Christ, faced the reality of his malignancy. Doctors didn't have to tell him that there was no known cure. He knew.

I could see for myself the physical, emotional, and mental deterioration brought on by the cancer's relentless march toward final conquest. Like a thief in the night, the quality of Mark's life steadily, quickly tip-toed into the shadows as death tightened its grip from one day to the next.

And the suffering—oh, the suffering! At times, it was so intense that he could not hold back the pleas for God to take his life. Mark did not choose the disease. It chose him. He was not intimidated by death, but the struggle and pain made him tired of living. In a predicament like this, doesn't self-imposed death become an acceptable, moral option?

Four Guidebook Answers—Through the Valley of the Shadow of Death

1. Shed life-suffocating notions.

Some I have heard include:

- Self-generated or other-generated or medically-generated death is the lesser of evils.
- In my case, death could be the most decent and humane of all choices.
- My life has no meaning if there is no substantive quality of life.
- If I keep on living, I create more problems and distress for my family.
- To extend my life is to extend my death.
- Death is the best way to keep grief in check and bring closure to stress.
- A good death is a basic human right.

Even if there is a thimble of truth in some of these notions, is there enough evidence to determine the life or death issue?

2. Fence suffering in.

After years of witnessing untold human misery, Albert Schweitzer, the mission pioneer and tireless physician, came to the conclusion that "pain is a more terrible lord . . . than death itself."[39]

There may be times when it looks like suffering holds all the cards. It seemed that way for Mark. Driven by pain, he questioned the value of life. That is understandable. In circumstances like that, no harm is done by the questions. But a fence needs to surround suffering from causes like a cancer.

A commitment to life I recommended seemed to help do that: "Suffering didn't have the power to give me life—suffering will not be given the power to decide my death."

It may also help to direct attention toward something that is free of suffering. New directions can be helpful. I admit, however, that this step requires a person to retain some ability to exercise it. At times, the intensity of suffering may prevent him from doing it. Therefore, it is something that can be done when there are rational times. Loved ones and friends may also be helpful. Become a stand-in for the one who suffers.

3. Activate faith-based relief.

In itself, suffering is neither good nor bad. It doesn't possess any sacred virtues or crown those who suffer with special graces. The sufferer's response determines the effect suffering has on the person—positive or negative.

In many cases, reduction and management—if not elimination—of pain is available, thank God! Medications and those who prescribe them are genuine favors from above.

If a person is terminally ill, reservations about the amount or potency should take a backseat to the person's need. Dr. C. S. Hill went so far as to say in the Journal of the American Medical Association that "all types of pain . . . are inadequately treated."[40]

Higher Level—Faith-Based Relief

I have known many people, including Mark, who tapped into one more available source of relief—God. The Almighty does not intend to substitute for physicians and medications, but to partner with them. When God entered the scene, suffering and pain medication were elevated to a higher level. The one who suffers can touch God through personal, private prayers. Others who care can touch God on behalf of the one who is suffering by quietly, silently praying for the person. It is also good to audibly pray with a suffering person.

And there may be occasions when a brief—no more than five minutes—time of compassion and prayer is conducted on behalf of the person. I call it a . . .

Service of Intervention

The service is God-centered, not pain-centered.

The focus is on the one who suffers, not the suffering.

The emphasis is on God who loves the person and works through physicians, scientists, health care professionals, and medications to bless people.

The objective is to seek divine blessing on the suffering person and trust God for it.

Participants in what I am talking about include the person who suffers and a significant other—a leader such as minister or spiritual advisor, believing family member or a friend. It may—in fact, at times should—include more people such as care partners (family members or close friends). On occasions, I have seen physicians, nurses, and other staff members join the service in a hospital room.

There are five ingredients in the very informal liturgy I used with Mark and others over a period of years:

- Accept assurance of God's love—two of my favorites are: "I [God] have loved you with a love that has always been and will never end" (Jer. 31:3) and "Nothing in all creation is able to separate us from the love of God revealed through Jesus Christ our Lord" (Rom. 8:35).
- Affirm God's power—"God has the power to help" (2 Chron. 25:8) and "God is strong, God is loving" (Ps. 62:11).

- Agree to God's involvement—"I [God] am with you; do not be dismayed, for I am your God. I will strengthen you and help you" (Isa. 41:10, NIV).
- Ask for God's help—a prayer that the medication will be effective and the body will be responsive to it. "God gives to those who ask" (Matt. 7:11).
- Acknowledge God's goodness—a word or sentence of thankfulness. "Give thanks to the Lord, for he is good; his love endures forever" (Ps. 106:1, NIV).

I have witnessed beneficial effects on those in need, however, it is very important to leave results to God and, in the words of a person who trusted that the Almighty is never wrong: "Praise the Lord whether conditions are good or bad" (Ps. 34:1).

4.   Settle the right to live vs. right to die question.

If a person has the right to live, then he has the right to die as he chooses, doesn't he? It is a logical question, but one that has an unstable foundation. No one of us chose, acquired, inherited, earned, negotiated, won, or deserved the right to life. It was given to us.

Life is a gift.

Now that we have life, the power of choice can be exercised in how, where, and when we live it—and whether we willfully end it. Still, death, like life, should be treated as a God-issue

IN RELATION TO.

Of all decisions a person could make, the one about living and dying is one that needs to be made in relation to God, oneself, family, and society. Everyone came into this world in relation to; each one should leave this world the same way. No one is authorized to act at his sole discretion.

Prayers like this one have been helpful: God, I belong to You. In waking, in sleeping, in consciousness, in unconsciousness, in pain, in pleasure, in times of fear, in times of faith, my life and days are in your hands. Amen.

Occasionally, loved ones and friends of a terminally ill person could offer this prayer on the person's behalf.

Mark lived a few more months and, although gaunt and bearing signs of a mighty struggle, died with a calm, peaceful appearance on his face.

Also, I am told, pain free.

Thank the Lord!

Permanent relief could have begun moments before he died.

As I finished a scripture, prayer, and personal encouragement, Mark's hand rested limply in mine. "Do you hear the music?" he asked softly. "David, do you hear the music?"

I knew Mark's appreciation for great hymns and his love to sing them—usually off key! I was also aware of his enjoyment of some southern gospel music (although he was a proud, life-long resident of the West Coast) and bluegrass with some country thrown in on the side. One of his holiday favorites was also mine—George Frederick Handel's magnificent "Messiah."

But music wasn't being piped into his room.

None could be heard from the hallway.

So, no, I didn't hear the music.

"I hear the music," Mark whispered as he eased into death.

I never heard it.

But who am I to doubt that he did!

It could have been coming from God's place welcoming Mark on his way home.

A. P. S.
(Author's Postscript)

Is it rare for terminally ill persons to think about ending their lives? Probably not—at least, not as rare as we think—or know. Environment, values, and faith combine to keep them silent about it. Mark didn't dwell on it, but he wasn't ashamed to bring up his death wish at times.

However, there is another scene in the picture.

Recently a psychiatrist and family physician—two friends in whom I have a lot of confidence—agreed that some of the debate over euthanasia may be a smokescreen for a desire to die that is caused by severe depression. In their experience, some patients who were seriously sick had thoughts about ending life. They felt the thoughts were driven by illness when depression had more to do with them. "And depression is treatable," the counselor said. Even so, a person can feel like Thomas Moore's "Last Rose of Summer."

According to Dr. David Clark, "Depressive episodes in the terminally ill are as responsive to treatment as depression in those not terminally ill."[41]

After a study of terminally ill patients, another group of specialists reported, "The striking feature of (our) results is that patients who had either desired premature death or contemplated suicide were judged to be suffering from clinical depressive illness . . . none who did not have clinical depression wished that death would come early."[42]

Death under such circumstances becomes an irreversible solution to a treatable problem.

Discussion Room

Agree	Disagree	
☐	☐	Mark wouldn't have suffered if it weren't God's will.
☐	☐	Pain can make a person stronger.
☐	☐	A person who suffers probably has brought it on himself or at least contributed to it.
☐	☐	If Mark had enough faith, he would have been cured.
☐	☐	In some cases, death is the lesser of evils.
☐	☐	If God were truly involved in every aspect of human life, there would not be suffering.
☐	☐	Heaven is a place where people of faith go after they die.

Agree	Disagree	
☐	☐	In heaven, people are pain-free.
☐	☐	We make our own heaven—it's here and now and is a state of mind.
☐	☐	Life ends at the grave.
☐	☐	Doctors, counselors and medical science are a waste of time and money. All anyone needs to do is trust God.
☐	☐	My life is my life. I should have the right to end it.
☐	☐	By living healthy, a person will avoid terminal diseases.
☐	☐	God heals all diseases.
☐	☐	If I become terminally ill, I will want to die.
☐	☐	God is good, even if there is suffering.

Life and Death Questions—Go Ahead, Ask

From whom has a person come?

The most exhaustive explanation science can offer is impressive, but falls short of a complete answer. After all, science is not a belief system. It is a tool that offers explanations for people to accept or reject.

Human arguments may be persuasive as far as they go, then they tumble like a spent meteorite. The fullest, and most plausible, answer is found in divine intelligence—God.

From my perspective, there is no other smart direction in which to go. Each person is the result of divine beginning.

Primarily, who owns a person's life?

The individual? A terminally ill person I knew justified the decision to take her own life with the assistance of a physician claiming, "It's mine. I can do this."

I would agree, if the person were the source of his or her own life. Otherwise, I don't buy it—not for a New York minute. In life, the first factor in ownership is source. Not possession, but source. Source trumps possession—always!

To what extent does a person have the right of life-or-death determination?

A person's basic right to make one's own decisions is God-given. Choice is one of the most thrilling advantages in being a person, but it is not singular and certainly not one that has been equally available in all areas of life.

For instance, you did not determine whether you were born, where you were born, into what family you were born, whether you were born male or female, and to what race, color, or cultural group you were born.

A person has the power to decide death and the timing of it for himself, but power is not a right. The right to decide when, where, and under what conditions the person lives or dies would be completely his own and absolute only if he created his own life. Here I am at source, again!

Isn't death with some semblance of dignity preferable to one that is dehumanizing?

Preferable, yes, but not guaranteed.

Besides, what contribution does self-induced or other-induced or medically-induced death make to basic human dignity?

Isn't freedom from suffering brought about through death better than extending suffering by prolonging life?

It is very clear to me that absence of suffering is certainly more desirable, but does it deserve the lofty right to determine life or death? If the power to decide is assigned to suffering, then the issue of intensity enters the picture.

What level of suffering has to be reached before suffering wisely decides it is time to die? I have known people for whom suffering, in spite of its atrocities, has benefited life by making life more significant—and bearable.

Is self-induced or other-induced or medically-initiated death worse than a person allowing oneself to die?

In my view, initiating death is a direct and deliberate act. On the other hand, simply allowing death to occur is a passive effect of withholding artificial methods of prolonging life.

Can you see a difference? I do.

Although the result—death—may be the same, the intent and process are strikingly different, as well as important. Allowing death does not assault dignity or the source of life.

Words of Wisdom from
Terminally Ill People I Have Known

You and I have responsibilities to family members or other decision-makers—also to God and ourselves—to spare them avoidable hardships, anxiety and, possibly, contentious disagreements, by making at least two key people aware of personal instructions before they are needed. Think of them as a . . .

My If List.

- If I become unable to make decisions that are in my best interests, or my family's interests—indicate who has primary responsibility and who has secondary responsibility. Add any other information that will provide guidance.
- If machines and other extraneous measures are required to keep me breathing indefinitely—specify what you want done about withdrawal or continuation of life-prolonging assistance under those conditions. Be definite and precise.
- If I am mentally alert and my family and I disagree about treatments, procedures, and a course of action—don't be hesitant to make known your preferences.

- If I cannot handle bills and other financial matters—be exact about who is granted power of attorney and *formalize the agreement.*
- If I require the services of a nursing home or care facility—make a wish list.
- If I were to die tomorrow—instructions and suggestions include:

  ◆ Make sure preferences for last rites or service are known
  ◆ The emphasis during the service (joy, gratitude, inspiration, comfort)
  ◆ Where it is to be held
  ◆ Who is to officiate
  ◆ Personal requests for the rite or service (music, scripture passages, etc.)
  ◆ Disposal of the body (burial, cremation or other).
  ◆ Any cap on burial expenses (your word could save a lot of money and, depending on financial resources, make an important difference for survivors at a time when reason may not be at its best for grieving decision-makers.)

Put the list in *writing* because the grass withers, the flower fades, and the memory fails. As a friend said when describing an experience from his past, "This is my memory of what happened and shouldn't be confused with what may have actually happened."

Although it doesn't qualify for the "My If List," Mark advised, "If there is something you really want to do before you die or somewhere you want to go, do it. Go without giving health a chance to slam the door."

Prayer for God's Suffering Children

Merciful God, when medication fails to bring relief, graciously squeeze in an abundance of love those who suffer. When ability to think rationally diminishes, hold them in strong arms of mercy. During times when life loses its attraction, bring something beautiful to their experience. When gutted by bad conditions, deepen the flow of goodness.

When ravages of decline seem unbearable, sustain with a presence that is supernatural. When there is thought about bringing life to a close, dispense a special grace to exercise good judgment.

You, faithful God, are the source for what is needed during life's trying hours.

Come alongside family members and friends with added grace to be life-givers while in the shadow of death.

Bless with success the scientists and researchers who seek cures for diseases. Increase strength to physicians, technicians, nurses, aides, ministers, and counselors who care for the terminally ill. In the spirit of Him who, in life and death, cares completely. Amen.

Good News

I feel as if my bones are out of joint . . . My God, why does it seem that You have abandoned me? Why is it that You seem so far away from bringing relief to me and do not hear the agonizing sounds of my suffering? . . . Your Heavenly Father knows that you need help especially now and will give you everything you need from day to day (Ps. 22:1, 14; Matt. 6:31).

---

Chapter Seven

*"It's behind closed doors,
so what's the big deal?"*

Luther, Attracted to Pornography—Yes, He Too, Was a Believer!

No other issue of morality has exploded with as much ferocity as pornography. It has moved from the outskirts of society into the mainstream and has become a growth industry that would fill Wall Street with envy. In America, for example, adult bookstores out number McDonalds. Not only has it become a billion dollar enterprise, revenues may be in the tens of billions. I am aware of a man in his mid-twenties who developed a website from which he reportedly is raking in profits of $1.5 million a month.

A high level commission on pornography referred to it as material that is "sexually explicit and intended primarily for the purpose of sexual arousal . . . (it is) devoid of any other apparent content or purpose."[43]

Extensive printed materials like magazines, video cassettes, motion pictures, and television combine to form a formidable onslaught of pornography. But the Internet has seen to it that a person no longer needs to go to a sleazy peep show, ridiculously misnamed gentlemen's club, or adult bookstore to enter its world. I already mentioned the website which is making its creator incredibly rich.

From anywhere on the planet, the Internet has put porn as close as a couple of clicks. Because of the privacy afforded by the Internet, a person could think that porn is a harm-free exercise, not to mention the user's right to make personal choices. Toss in the idea that those who provide it are engaging in freedom of speech and the argument seems to become irrefutable. As long as children are not involved, what is the problem?

It's behind closed doors, Luther thought, *so what's the big deal?*

The attraction to porn doesn't discriminate based on race, color, language, economic ability, or residence—not even age. Not long ago, a sixteen-year-old high school student who lives in America's down-home Midwest wrote to the famous advice columnist, Dear Abby. "I'm friendly, cheerful, religious, and an honors student. I am also addicted to pornography."[44] She explained that for several years, she has been in and out of it and promises herself that she will stop it. But, after a few months of being clean, she starts again.

Luther had a similar experience.

He really was a likeable person, successful at what he did, and well thought of in the community. His family was important to him. He had a pleasant personality and a compassionate heart. Luther would have given you the shirt off his back, if you needed it. Moreover, he professed to be a follower of Christ and as far as people could tell, he lived like one. He went to church regularly. Those who attended enjoyed being greeted by him; he was one of the best ushers you would find anywhere. People were impressed with his winsome smile and warm greeting.

But the porn demon ran wild on the inside. "It fascinated me," he admitted, "and grew on me."

It isn't uncommon for people to cover their behavior in a secrecy rivaling national security. Or try to.

True or False Quiz—No Room to Fudge

1. As a porn user, I'm aware that I use those who are featured in the materials for self-stimulation, self-gratification and selfish pleasure, but the use of it is okay. After all, that's the reason for the materials.
   True.

You are using people, but the use is all about you. That is wrong. Anything that is all about you is galling self-centeredness and would be better treated as a social, moral, and spiritual bubonic plague.

2. The use of others to achieve the purposes for the materials doesn't include one-on-one interaction. In the context of use, the absence of interaction is okay.
   False.
   Use of others with zero interaction is not okay due to the highly personal nature of sexual activity, the perimeters within which it satisfies a basic desire, as well as need, and the depth of love it is intended to express. The lack of inter-action betrays a "Thing Mentality" toward the other person; in pornography, the other person is treated as an object that can be used.

3. I have to turn to porn to experience satisfaction.
   False.
   Anything so blatantly self-absorbing that uses others callously and essentially treats them as objects rather than persons is way off any social, emotional, and spiritual center. Therefore, it is incapable of producing the highest level of gratification.

4. My use of porn is no one's business except mine.
   False.
   When another person, any other person, is used, or influenced, or treated, or thought of in a disrespectful way, it becomes the business of at least one other person—that person—in addition to the one doing it.

5. Watching and reading porn is a legitimate way to channel my excessive sex drive without hurting anyone.
   False.
   In addition to the one using porn, someone, somewhere, in some way—physically, emotionally, socially, or spiritually—

is being harmed by the activity including those who produce and sell the product.

6. Experiencing pleasure is basic to a balance, fulfilled life.
False.
Pleasure contributes to a fulfilled life. It is not basic to life, and it isn't the cause behind life. Pleasure is *a* fruit, not *the* root. It is not even a root. Think of pleasure as result rather than cause.

7. The way I use pornography isn't really a moral question.
True . . . if the One who made you has not provided standards for behavior in public and private life that is good for you and good for all.
False . . . if the One who is behind your life offers a way of life that blesses you and those your life touches.

8. My use of porn doesn't contribute to any serious social issue either. If there is a negative impact, it is blown way out of proportion. After all, it's only me.
False.
Any activity, whether thought of as good, bad or with indifference, affects society to some extent, even when it is practiced by no more than two persons. Pornography involves at least two people—the used and the user.

Five Guidebook Answers— Follow the Ion Trail to Sunshine

1. Aversion.

In an attempt to explain his use of pornography, a man once said, "I was born with sex drive in overdrive." Not really (and I think he knew it). There may be a proclivity in favor of types of behavior which is at odds with a person's best interests, but behavior is not who a person is. Behavior is what a person does—the way one acts.

Attraction to a Type of Behavior Is Acquired, Not Required!

It is instilled, not inborn. As I see it, pornographic behavior—whether by a user or purveyor—is the "what" that reflects who the person is. In this scenario, the "what" is pornographic activity by the "who," the person doing it. The behavior happens *because* a person is wayward. Behavior is always because. However, there is no need to be disheartened. Negative behavior can be averted!

2. Subversion.

If an attraction that leads to harmful behavior is acquired, not required, the attraction can be subverted—overthrown—by shifting the attraction to positive behavior. Furthermore, an attraction once acquired by a person, then lost, can be reacquired.

FOR EVERY MINUS, THERE IS A PLUS!

Mired in a maze of "don't, thou shalt not, thee must not, woe if thou dost," people fail to recognize that a person loses nothing of value by setting aside nothing of value. In fact, he gains something of value by getting rid of nothing of value or lesser value.

I see this mighty principle from the story of Jesus in which He says to followers, "Anyone who does what I do follows me and my Father honors anyone who does what I do" (John 12:26).

FOR EVERY LOSS, A GAIN—AND MORE!

Not only is there a gain for every loss, there is a gain plus *added value*. For instance, overthrowing negative behavior by positive behavior brings more satisfying and fortifying results such as self-respect, a wholesome frame of mind, a healthier attitude toward others, and a justifiable sense of pride

The pursuit of pleasure through pornography may be beyond a person's control, but it is not uncontrollable. Although this isn't the total answer, directing mental and emotional energies toward other things can reinforce success over the addiction.

THINK BEFORE YOU SINK!

Think about disadvantages of pornographic behavior before turning to it, watching it, reading it, and sitting through it. Shift your attention away from it and focus on positives that strengthen character and build a wholesome self-image.

3. Desertion.

During my service in Naval Aviation, I learned that desertion is referred to as AWOL—Away Without Leave. To overcome errant behavior like pornography, desertion means to leave the loser's I-Me Standard (behavior predominantly based on the individual, "me") on the sideline in favor of the Me-Them Rule (behavior that is enriching to oneself and others). Start by answering two important questions:

"Is what I want to do good for me?" If yes, it is good for family members, friends, and society. If no, it is hurtful for everyone.

"Is what I want to do detrimental to me?" If yes, then it is also detrimental to them. There is no way for a person to say that he is completely an island unto oneself and keep a straight face.

Behavior Based on the Me-Them Rule
Blesses Everyone Touched by the Behavior.

No one is left behind by behavior that reflects the Me-Them Rule in daily life. This rule insists that everyone connected to or affected in any way by pornographic behavior has personal worth to God. This includes you, your family, others whose lives are in touch with your life and, yes, the persons featured in the porn and those who provide it.

God deemed each one of sufficient significance to grant the gift of life, the opportunity to uniquely experience the grandeur of being, the call to participate in the joys of senses, and the invitation to redeemed life.

4. Insertion.

A pursuit of pleasure through pornography may be out of control. Beyond a person's control, however, it is not uncontrollable. But there is more to bringing it under control than emptying the mind of thoughts about it and engaging in warfare with the desire for it. One of the tools by which pornography can be overcome is to insert thoughts and conditions that offer something of greater value. A friend of mine illustrates what I am talking about. After being a pornie for fifteen years, he decided to quit.

"I was serious," he said, "and determined to give it my best shot. But I wasn't successful until I filled my mind with thoughts that weren't about pornography."

At the times when he usually got into it, such as late at night, or when he was out of town, or at home alone, he made it a point to insert thoughts other than pornography.

"When thoughts and feelings began to say 'here's your chance to use it,' I'd think about how blessed I am, what a great time to be alive, the work I am privileged to do, how sacred life is, how long I want it to last, how healthy I would like to be, and advantages of being porn-free."

In a poignant story in the Gospel, Jesus made it clear that empty space will not remain empty when He talked about an evil spirit leaving a man then returned to find the man's house empty. The demon occupied the house again and invited more demons to join him; the man's final condition was then worse than before the demon left the first time (see Luke 11:24–26).

When the inclination to porn begins to raise its ugly head, quickly overcome the desire by changing your mental scenery. Deny the attraction continued exposure in your mind. Cut off its parade before it gets started.

5. Exertion.

Use of pornography is a negative response to the God-given capacity for sexual satisfaction. Combating it successfully includes positive efforts.

I mentioned the man who wanted to break free from pornography. He confirmed that without exerting effort to overcome the demon, he would have failed. When he saw pictures of scantily clad women, he would look away. When conversation began to drift in that direction, he removed himself from it. When the urge to use porn was strong, he would read audibly a passage from the Bible. Blinking the eyes in rapid succession for a few moments also helped to break a thought pattern.

There is no substitute for effort. Without it, all other steps become null and void. In fact, according to the apostle James, even faith without works is dead (James 2:20).

However, as important as the will to win is—as well as moral alertness, holy intentions, consecrated desires, redeeming objectives, and enlightened hopes—winning takes more than any of these. In fact it takes more than all of them combined. Effort with God's power behind it makes the difference. The difference is deliverance from the demon through transformation.

How did Luther fare?

Listen while he answers.

Five Super Ds

Desire—"I found ways to change what I wanted—porn—by focusing on interests that were good for me and those around me. Over time, my wants changed."

Development—"I also found that a one-time-for-all-time commitment didn't work for me. Rather than waste physical, emotional, and spiritual capital on porn, I continued to develop interests to occupy the time previously taken up by pornography. I'm still at it."

Destiny—"I had to reconnect with my purpose for being on earth. I think everyone has a purpose and when it is lost or pushed aside, a person stumbles."

Divine—"I needed the direct, personal involvement of God specifically in regards to this issue in my life. I think I've been a Christian, at least since college days, but I let this area of my life slip away from it."

Devotion—"I also found that I needed to submit myself and this shortcoming particularly to the Lord. I was told that it would put in play the resources of the supernatural to where I was like I was. That's true. I've had to renew devotion often."

I am sure that the demon would still be loose in Luther's life were it not for the Super Ds.

I believe Luther would shout, "You're right, brother, you're right!"

A. P. S.
(Author's Postscript)

A man told me that he began to delve into pornography after his relationship with his wife fizzled. "It didn't seem that we were attracted to one another anymore. It never became a contentious issue," he explained, matter-of-factly. "The desire for intimacy with each other faded away."

To the credit of both husband and wife, they found that it's possible for relationship to be reestablished.

On the other hand, diminished sexual satisfaction is a result of using pornography. In one study, researchers discovered that porn users became unhappy with their partner's affection, appearance, curiosity, and performance.[44] Furthermore, users often emphasized the sexual act itself without considering the importance of emotional involvement.

I have not found any objective scientific study to indicate that pornography has redeeming value.

Discussion Room

Agree	Disagree	
☐	☐	Pornography is a freedom of speech issue.
☐	☐	What worked for Luther won't work for everyone.
☐	☐	As long as there are sinful people, there will be pornography.
☐	☐	The porn problem, if there is one, cannot be solved.
☐	☐	A genuine follower of Christ will avoid pornography.
☐	☐	If you can't whip 'em, join 'em—it would be better to legalize and regulate pornography.
☐	☐	My church should be more outspoken about pornography.
☐	☐	"If it's not my itch, I don't scratch"—I'm not affected by porn, so I don't see a need to get involved.
☐	☐	Once a porn addict, always a porn addict.
☐	☐	The spouse should leave a porn user.
☐	☐	Pornography is a fantasy world—a world divorced from reality.
☐	☐	As long as pornography doesn't create social and crime problems, don't dither over it.
☐	☐	Never shall the twain meet—porn and spirituality have nothing to do with one another.
☐	☐	God loves a porn user, in spite of his faults.

Voices from the Other Side—Ex-Porn Users

- "It began as a recreational exercise and grew to the point where I began to look for any opportunity to find porn on the Internet."
- "I didn't want my spouse or children to catch me, so I made sure they were gone or asleep. Late one night, my six-year-old daughter walked in on me. She didn't catch on to what I was doing, but it still troubled me."
- "I travel a lot in my job and started watching adult movies available in the hotel room."
- "Women are porn users, too, and I was one of them."
- "It led me to separate myself from my family. I wasn't happy with them. They aggravated me."
- "My spouse had suspicions. She confirmed them when she found my user name and password to access porn sites. I was humiliated and hurt. So was she."
- "Unexplained charges started appearing on credit cards (porn sites charge fees). It alerted my spouse to a problem."
- "My spouse was a very wise (and believing) person. She knew I wouldn't change (porn use) by nagging and spying on me."
- "We (husband and wife) found that a love lost can be a love regained. I'll be forever glad that she didn't kick me out."
- "For a fact, I know there is life beyond pornography—free from guilt, false hopes, and hypocrisy. It's not possible to describe how much better I feel with myself."

Prayer for Deliverance

All-knowing God, from whom is mercy that has no end, visit those to whom pornography is appealing with help to see that any gratification it offers is only momentary. May they recognize that such use of the gift of time degrades their attitude, outlook, and perception of themselves and the opposite sex.

Lift the fog surrounding their souls so that they can see the corruption in their behavior and the silent hurt it causes to those who are dear to them. Grant the sense to acknowledge that pornography traumatizes character. Instill within them a more compelling appreciation for life and beauty.

Lord of grace, guidance is available to ways that better satisfy sexual desires. Strength to use powers of imagination profitably is close by. Pry open their deepest self to receive this guidance and strength, discover the gold mine found in a clean mind, and experience the joy that comes from defeating something which has defeated them.

Cause them to feel an unstoppable compulsion to trust themselves and their need to Your transforming power. In the name of Him in whom there is freedom. Amen.

Good News

What is my life? It is like a cloud which can be seen only for a short while, then poof, it is gone . . . Lord, cleanse me from hidden faults. Don't let them control me; only then will I be free (James 4:4; Ps. 19:12–13).

Chapter Eight

*"I have a right to be happy—if
not at home, then elsewhere."*

Lonnie, Extramarital Affair—Of Course, He Knew Better!

He wasn't a moral imbecile. And he was no loose cannon or frisky young stallion. However, none of these kept Lonnie from a secret love affair with a friend of the family.

What first prompted him to come to me about it?

Second thoughts about how he fell into it?

Could it have been guilt?

Possibly, fear of financial losses (affairs have been known to be very costly)?

Or the no-nonsense policy of a boss who had a short fuse for excursions like this? From experience, many managers have found that attitude, performance, and the company's profit sheet have been adversely affected by employees in extramarital relationships.

Was it the wellbeing of children?

A revolution of his values?

Spiritual rumblings (he was known as a Christian)?

He could have come due to slumping self-esteem, or outside influences like drugs and alcohol, or during one of life's dramatic phase changes such as the birth of a child, career adjustment, entry into the thirty-something, forty-something, fifty-something crowd, or empty nest syndrome.

But none of these fit him. Whatever the reason behind it, Lonnie came to me a bit apprehensive and nervous, but not timidly.

Dr. Willard Harley, the well-known counselor and best-selling author, described an affair as a relationship that satisfies a need not met in marriage.[45] Due to popular perception, it may be surprising to hear that the need is not necessarily of a physical nature—at least, not in the beginning. A substantial body of research indicates that as little as 10 percent of the time is a desire for intimacy involved.[46] Yet, estimates of infidelity in America have ranged from 20 –70 percent.

Fifteen Reasons for Marriage Treason

Some of the causes I've been told include:

- Loneliness—"We lived in the same house and I was surrounded by people, but I felt separated from my spouse. It chewed through my soul."
- Lost love—"Intimacy at home disappeared."
- New frontier—"I wanted to see what it was like on the other side of the fence."
- Lack of fulfillment—"There's got to be more for me than what I'm getting in my marriage."
- Bravado—"I suppose I felt a need to prove that I still had the right stuff."
- Challenge—"The call of the chase got the best of me."
- Appeal—"She was irresistible."
- Admiration—"He was emotionally satisfying and intellectually stimulating."
- Incompatibility—"We (husband and wife) didn't see eye to eye on anything . . . the perfect misfits."
- Boredom—"My life was so routine. I needed to break out of the rut."
- Attention—"I didn't get it at home."
- Sexual appetite—"I thought I had more sexual drive than one person could satisfy."

- Down the totem pole affliction—"At home, I felt I wasn't important."
- Disability or illness—"My spouse was no longer able to make love."
- Don't know—"I didn't intend to cheat, never in a million years. Why I did it? I don't have a clue. It just happened."

Forces in society add their two cents worth by routinely treating affairs as normal as ice cream and apple pie at the community picnic. From movies, novels, soap operas, and TV shows, it is easy to get the impression that the smart life is impossible apart from a relationship with women so beautiful that they blow your socks off and men who are perfect specimens of Mr. Universe. If not controlled, the messages oozing from them soften a person's defenses.

Those involved in secret love affairs may be the nicest people, handsome, attractive, fun, considerate, educated, polite, successful, and religious—at least in name. On the other hand, they may not be any of these.

One of the stark realities about human nature is the capacity for anyone to develop an outside-of-marriage love. A respected counselor stated it bluntly: "We all are wired to have an affair. If you don't think it can happen to you . . . you are particularly vulnerable."[47] Color, race, language, status, education, poverty, wealth, religion—nothing completely immunizes a person against the possibility. It isn't far-fetched to think that anyone reading these lines, faithful believers and all, could honestly admit, "Except for the grace of God . . ."

Six Guidebook Answers— Rebirth of Happiness

1. Review cause.

As with most problems, the path to overcoming infidelity begins with identifying what is behind it. The cause could be a threatening sense of entitlement, "I have a right to be happy—if not at home, then elsewhere." This attitude has become more acceptable in many cultures, especially North America and Europe. Its throne room is saturated with *Mighty I,* a well-documented loser.

One or more of the Reasons For Marriage Treason that I have outlined could be the culprit. Usually, however, there is a combination of reasons. Peggy Vaughan, recognized as an authority on marital relationships, claims that there is no one single reason.[48] On the other hand, maybe none these reason applies. What are some others?

Emotional detachment—living together, but spiritually divorced.
Two careers—both spouses working outside the home, the role of provider and homemaker has been put aside and dependence on each other has tanked out.
Improbable expectations—holding your spouse to lofty, unattainable ideals.
Faulty love notion—when it becomes apparent that love doesn't always conquer all.
Failed love potion—a spouse who practices abstinence. A wife told me that her husband's wanderings had her tacit approval: "I didn't want sexual contact of any kind."
Unresolved problems—like money (especially lack of it), extended family (in-laws, for sure), death of a child, differences about number of children, role of husband and wife, and even religion.
Strangulation—failure to give enough for the marriage to prosper.
Childishness—immaturity when one or both marriage partners act like the forty-year-old who still didn't know what he wanted to be when he grew up.

A bold review of the cause is necessary unless the person wants to be like a headless horseman who rides off in all directions to nowhere. It also wouldn't hurt to consider the advice of Dr. Phil McGraw, the popular TV personality and counselor: "Don't try to make sense out of non-sense."[49]

2. Reconsider justification.
Someone in an extramarital affair is desperate to find a supporting cast of characters saying that it is okay. Jot down everyone that comes to mind and, using three categories, rate them based on the impact they have.

Really Significant—Major impact affecting emotional, mental, social, professional, and spiritual health. God has made each person with a need for affection, security, friendship, companionship, and fulfillment. Loss of any of these may nudge a person into thinking an affair is acceptable.

Quite Influential—Persuasive, but do not rise to the level of *Really Significant*. For example, "It fills a need at the moment."

Just Because—Enticement, convenience, desire, temporary rendezvous, and "it's there for the taking and I could take it" are examples.

Now complete this sentence: "It is okay for me to have a secret love since_____."

Someone told me that he couldn't complete the sentence. "Looking at what I had determined to be reasons for it, my mind went blank. I had to be honest. I couldn't find any justification I could continue to live with."

3. Recalculate the cost.

Most of us have heard the saying, "Nothing in life is free." An extramarital affair is no exception. In fact, the price a person pays includes dollars and cents such as additional expenses necessary to keep it going, potential lawsuits, divorce and alimony or prior family support. But the cost doesn't stop there. I have observed that the tab includes:

Emotional—a lost sense of well being. What could start with promise often leaves an empty shell and remorse.
Fear—of being found out.
Extra Energy—required to keep it going.
Effort—planning and arrangements necessary to be together.
Risk—of embarrassment and humiliation.
Lost Integrity—diluted honor and honesty.
Exposure to Consequences—a year from now, five years, ten years. It is surprising how often fully grown people act in non-grown-up ways. A secret love is one of those times. I remember a woman who admitted that she had not given the first thought to future consequences for

her romantic tryst. "Apparently," she said, "I was so absorbed with the moment that tomorrow didn't rate a blip on the radar screen. At least, not as big as it should." In reflection she thought, "That was really childish, wasn't it?"

Dr. Harley spoke from experience with countless cases of infidelity when he shared that the expense of it is incalculable on the person, spouse, children, extended family members, and friends.[50]

4. Retire from the affair.

I have observed that behavior *always*—always—helps or hinders in finding the solution. In human relationships, a person will not completely behave oneself into happiness, but the way he behaves will make a difference like nothing else will.

Behavior is the result of choices, but choice is like a two-sided coin. Let's call one side *Intent*—action based on deliberate, willful decision. In this case, the behavior is intentional.

Joshua is one of my favorite people in the Old Testament. He called the ancient Hebrews to choose to follow God faithfully and went so far as to say that if that seemed unreasonable, decide whomever or whatever they wished, then added, "But as for me and my family, we will serve the Lord" (Josh. 24:15, LB). That was bold, uncorrupted choice by intent.

Let's call the other side of the coin *Default*—action without any particular, conscious decision. It is like, "This just happened" . . . "It happened without my saying yes."

After St. Paul persuasively voiced his faith in the presence of Agrippa, the king responded, "You almost convince me to become a follower of Jesus" (Acts 26:28). The record of this encounter mentions that the king and his entourage left the room—nothing else to indicate that he responded with a yes or no. Nothing was his decision. It was made by default.

Do not be conned into thinking that choice by default is not a choice or that choice by default comes without accountability. Choice by default is still a choice.

An extramarital affair does not end unless at least one of the persons involved makes a choice that in effect says, "Enough!" "Finito!" "I'm done with it!" "It's over!" A saying reminiscent of one liners by the famous baseball catcher, Yogi Berra, claims that something is not over until the large lady sings. In this situation, call on the large lady to sing.

Usually, retirement means an end to something such as retiring a debt or retiring from activities of the day. In human interaction, a more complete meaning of the word is an end to something in favor of beginning something else.

Recently, a friend retired from a long and productive career in the insurance business. It marked the close of a lifelong commitment to helping and serving people in a professional capacity. Since then, he has doubled his efforts on behalf of his church and people of need in the community.

Retirement from a secret love affair is the ending of something which ultimately, if not sooner, is a slam dunk for pain. It requires action. The reward for positive action is a happier "me"—the one involved in the affair—and "us"—others affected by the affair, like the companion in infidelity, and family members of both persons.

5. Recommit to solution.

Think about the "us" I have mentioned. Happiness in relationship is NOT all about you—it includes you, but much more than you—and invokes the . . .

Thee-We-Me Principle

for everyday life.

An out-of-marriage love connection betrays a breakdown of personal moral focus. The wall of morality is in need of repair. The authentic source for what is needed to repair the wall is the one who gives life and makes genuine fulfillment possible—God. Therefore, the divine is the beginning point in this equation.

A face-to-face with the Almighty will do. Seekers will find the welcome mat is out. They can take comfort in believing that they aren't the first ones to come with the secret love problem, and that God has proven credentials in dealing with the situation.

"We" in the equation are others most directly involved, specifically the love partner. If advisable, share the course of action with him or her in hope of coming to a shared agreement. If the other person will not cooperate, decisive unilateral action works effectively.

What about "me"? A person is a winner when Thee-We dynamics are released in his life. "Thee" instead of "I" takes over the throne. "We" is recognition of the intrinsic value and importance of others. Through Thee-We, "Me" is elevated to the higher purpose for which you were given life, breath, and being.

I feel the principle is reflected in the Gospel account when Jesus called some people to become disciples. "Come after me and I will help you to become all that you can be" (Matt. 4:19). Coupled with another declaration of Jesus, it is crystal clear. "No one leaves anything or anyone in pursuit of fulfilling his God-given destiny who will not receive much more in the present life and eternal life" (Luke 18:29–30).

When a person does the right thing, no one loses—no one! The opportunity to make things right remains available for anyone who has possession of breath, abilities, possibilities, and destination.

The door to a solution is opened with keys like responsibility, talk, support from others, and forgiveness. Time is also an important element. As Dr. McGraw advises, "Time doesn't heal. What is done with time heals."[51]

6. Rejoice.

Put the power of words to use by using words with joyful overtones. Goodness, self-control, success, hope, forgiveness, newness, confidence, freedom, faith, grace, patience, endurance, and strength are among them. Form a sentence of the day using one of the words for that day. Repeat the sentence often throughout the day.

In addition, notice little things that deserve passing appreciation: a flower, cloud, bird, smile, or a warm greeting. Positive words and restorative action bring good results for everyone.

Did they for Lonnie?

Did he and his wife live happily ever after?

Well, no—not exactly!

Just as he was recovering from his own indiscretion, his wife started a secret love affair with a single man, filed for divorce, married him, and moved to another state. Lonnie remembered his extramarital rendezvous, felt the pain, and held his head up. He would not surrender to his past and refused to be defeated.

And he is glad that he did—very glad.

So is God!

A. P. S.
(Author's Postscript)

Amazingly, Lonnie's affair remained unknown to his wife and other family members. Did he have the responsibility to tell them? Would it have been better for them—and him? I did not consider it to be in anyone's best interests for him to divulge his indiscretion. On the other hand, if the subject came up, I suggested that he not try to hide or skirt the truth and certainly not to run from it. Instead:

Confess—admit to the affair.
Express—plainly share regrets and sorrow that it happened and ask
forgiveness.
Redress—as much as possible, make relationships right.
Bless—show by word and deed a life that is now affair-free.

Regardless of outcome, it is important to believe that there is life after closing out a secret love. A person can make it through any second thoughts, numbness, wandering, longings, depression, and other mood swings. Redirecting energies, re-routing interests, and re-establishing life-building bonds help negotiate the recovery process. Languishing in second, third or fourth thoughts negate it.

After his divorce, Lonnie went through a period of grief as real as losing a loved one. He managed to last through it and discovered a richness he could not, in his brightest moments, drum up singlehandedly for himself—something to truly live for, standards to live by, work, play, leisure, attachment, connection, reward, relationship, love, and romance. He became more aware of the difference these qualities make in a person's life, the loss he feels when they are absent, and what an individual will do in search of them. In time, another person entered his life (not the one with whom he had an affair). They married and are enjoying the caliber of relationship they deserve.

Discussion Room

Agree	Disagree	
☐	☐	Everyone needs to feel that he or she is valued, cherished, and respected.
☐	☐	If Lonnie and his wife really loved each other, he wouldn't have had an extramarital affair.
☐	☐	It's okay to show shock, rage, shame, and remorse when an affair becomes public.
☐	☐	The Bible is the only guide a person needs.
☐	☐	The way humans are made, physical attraction is as natural as peaches and cream.
☐	☐	Exclusiveness in marriage is too much to ask.
☐	☐	To clear the deck, Lonnie should have told his wife about the affair.
☐	☐	A husband or wife should be understanding and accommodating, if a spouse is unable to be intimate due to illness, a handicap, or emotional problem.
☐	☐	When a spouse is denied intimacy, it's okay to find it with another person.
☐	☐	The best way to determine how a person will act in the future is to base it on how he or she has acted in the past.
☐	☐	If Lonnie's wife had known about the affair, the best course of action for her would have been to forgive and forget.

Agree	Disagree	
☐	☐	The wife or husband of a person who has had an affair has the obligation to help her or him get over it.
☐	☐	No one ever completely gets over an infidelity—not really!
☐	☐	A person cannot work on the affair while he or she is still having it.
☐	☐	God loves an unfaithful person, too.
☐	☐	C. S. Lewis is right: A person is never too old to set another goal or to dream a new dream.[52]

Words of Wisdom from Some Who've Been There, Done That

- The affair wasn't worth the emotional and spiritual cost.
- My spouse was no longer interested in intimacy, and I was. After two years, I felt I had a right to find another partner. It would have been better to work on the problem. We didn't.
- I felt God would understand. God did understand me, but I found that God didn't approve my behavior.
- I've enjoyed every minute of my affair. He's my love. No regrets here, not yet.
- I wasn't careful on business trips [with associates of the opposite sex]. Wish I had been.
- When I got into the affair, I didn't give a second thought to any consequences. A big mistake!
- I wasn't the one who pushed it. He was the aggressor. Sorry I didn't cut him off.
- I "went out for hamburger" and lost the "steak" at home. (A reference to fidelity by award-winning actor, Paul Newman, who told a reporter, "Why go out for hamburger when I can have steak at home?")

- The affair wasn't all it was cracked up to be.
- I'm in an affair, but it's temporary. I don't think he knows yet.

Watch Out—Danger Ahead!

Pickings are ripe for an extramarital affair if a husband and wife:

- Quit sharing goals and dreaming new dreams.
- Suspicions and distrust go unresolved.
- Don't talk about problems.
- Begin to doubt a future together.
- Fail to support each other.
- "I love you" and "I need you" go unspoken.
- Give up attempts to solve problems.
- "Me" becomes more important than "we."
- Settle for the way "things are" in the marriage—the status quo.
- Differences are allowed to fester.
- Fail to set aside time exclusively for one another.
- Opportunities to grow are refused.
- Children and extended family members become more important than each other.
- Refuse to allow space for personal interests.
- Allowances aren't made for one another's shortcomings.
- Daily life dwells on complaints.
- Fault-finding is excessive.
- Impulses aren't controlled.
- Crises are unresolved.
- Someone other than the wife or husband is thought to be more appropriate.
- Attention is not devoted to the marriage.
- Spiritual integrity is compromised.

Prayer for Rebirth of Happiness

Holy God, I praise You for understanding the human need for special people with whom to share life and Your provision to satisfy the need.

Come, O faithful One, to those who are married but have another love. Cover them with the help needed to recognize that the affair is disrespectful of themselves, their partners, and their families.

Forgiving Savior, lead them to confess that the relationship is abusive spiritually, emotionally, mentally, and socially to everyone touched by it. Grant courage to face the truth that a wrong act can never be right and bring them to the decision that a wrong like theirs can be corrected in a way that benefits everyone.

Bless with humility to depend on You for power to take the next step toward the independence and wholeness You have for them. In the name of the One who loves us in spite of ourselves. Amen.

Good News

Free me from the trap that I am in, O God of truth . . . What is gained if I do everything my heart desires, but forfeit life? . . . God will send His angel to shut the mouth of the lion in your midst (Ps. 31:4, 5; Mark 8:36; Dan. 6:22).

Chapter Nine

He succeeded when he should have
failed—wouldn't it have been better to fail?

E. J. Took His Own Life—and Derrick Tried Too

E. J. wasn't from the wrong side of the tracks. Professionals have found depression, bipolar disorder, schizophrenia, and situations that appear to be overwhelming are some of the forces that lead a person to take his life. But none of these was obvious with E. J. His career seemed be on the upside. His family loved him. Money worries didn't seem to bother him, and he was free from suffering and other serious physical problems.

The sixty-plus crowd is one of two groups with the highest (and most successful) rate of self-destruction. However, age didn't apply to E. J. He wasn't yet in the fabulous forties. Furthermore, the last time we talked, he acted positive about his faith.

Still, he took his life.

It baffles me to this day.

I suppose there may have been some chaotic spirit meandering through E. J.'s mind pitting him against himself. Conflicts that made him feel powerless could have been raging inside. Maybe devils shook his confidence and put subordinates in control causing him to feel overwhelmed by an illusion that if he were dead things would be better.

We'll never know.

But there is no quibbling about one fact: he succeeded.

Self-initiated death is the eleventh leading cause of death among Americans—the figure is higher in some other western nations. Tens of thousands ended their own lives last year, hundreds of thousands were treated in emergency rooms, and hundreds of thousands more were hospitalized for self-inflicted injuries. The cost in dollars and cents is staggering. According to the U. S. Department of Health & Human Services, it topped $33 billion last year.[53]

It is obvious that in addition to the emotional and practical toll on families and communities, it has become a serious social problem with far-reaching implications.

Directly Intentional—Directly Unintentional

As I see it, suicide is two dimensional. It may be directly intentional. For example, a gunshot (the most common method among men), an overdose, a slashed artery, a dose of poison, or a deliberate car wreck.

On the other hand, it may be directly unintentional. For instance, lifestyles which contribute firsthand to death including alcoholism, drug addictions, excessive and harmful eating habits, and use of tobacco products are the by-products of disrespect for the body and life. They represent failure to accept both as gifts.

Aside from severe mental illness, the most dominant cause of self-inflicted death cannot be seen or touched.

It is such a loss of purpose for living that death becomes an agreeable course of action.

I didn't have the opportunity to share any thoughts that may have helped E. J. I was like all the others who had no idea that he was considering suicide. But since then I have made it my business to pay closer attention to people who may be thinking about it, as well as to the survivors like Derrick who tried to take his life.

Derrick made a serious effort, but "I bungled it," he admitted. Once he was full of hope for life, the community, and humanity in general. "I was pretty sure that problems could be solved. The longer I lived, though, the more pessimistic I became. Then I lost all hope." Despair rubbed off on his personal and family life to the extent that he felt life was a sham.

Seven Guidebook Answers— a Roadmap to Revitalization

1. Thank God for success denied.

Edward George Bulwer-Lytton, the popular eighteenth century poet, wrote,

> In the lexicon of youth, which fate reserves
> For a bright manhood, there is no such word
> As "fail."[54]

But, in some instances, there is success in a failed suicide attempt. Success in self-destruction would actually constitute a failure. Some who try to destroy themselves wish they had succeeded, but failure is no time to cry over spilled milk! It is a golden opportunity to exercise a powerful spiritual fact: "Give thanks . . . this is God's plan for you" (1 Thess. 5:18).

GOD DOESN'T HOLD A FAILED ATTEMPT AGAINST A PERSON!

The basic reason someone can be thankful for an unsuccessful suicide attempt is the Lord's attitude toward the person. Not even a tiny drop of divinely-given potential has been taken away—not one! The unsuccessful incident can be dispensed to the personal Land of Left Behind, and be no more.

2. Recognize thieves of desire to live.

The attack may begin with a single robber. However, it is usually joined by others, one at a time, until there is a ruthless gang pressing the battle. What are some of these bandits?

- Questionable Usefulness—"The blast in life is past. The best days are behind me."
- Adversity—"It's one problem after the other. Why don't I get some relief?"

111

- Anonymous Attacks on Life's Little Pleasures—"I don't like living anymore. Sometimes I don't know why."
- Mishandled Disappointments—"I don't deserve what happened to me. I tried to deal with it, but to no avail."
- Unchecked Cynicism—"Life is no longer what it was cracked up to be."
- Doubtful Worth—"I am so insignificant. What difference do I make?"

Adversity and Doubtful Worth often are at the front of the gang.

Armed with recognition, a person is better equipped to counter attack.

3. Apply the Step Ladder Formula to problems.

When a person feels powerless in the face of problems, he begins to suffer the Humpty Dumpty Syndrome. Remember the words of the kindergarten rhyme?

> Humpty Dumpty sat on a wall,
> Humpty Dumpty had a great fall.
> All the king's horses and all the king's men,
> Couldn't put Humpty together again.[55]

If problems are perceived to be serious enough for long enough, they threaten one's life. The Step Ladder Formula has been helpful:

Step A—This problem has come, but this problem will go.
Step B—I will do what I can about it.
Step C—I will accept the help I need.
Step D—I will adjust to what cannot be changed.
Step E—I will make an adjustment that could help avoid a similar problem in the future.

4. Touch a dandelion.

That is the way my friend, Clyde, worded it. During growing up years, he tended to let opportunities and events that weren't spectacular go unnoticed. Many of us do the same. "I'm bored," he would complain. "Each time I'd say that, my mother would reply, 'Go touch a dandelion'" which grew profusely where they lived. "Her point was to pay attention to little pleasures. After becoming an adult, I began to let life chew me up. I forgot to 'go touch a dandelion.'"

The greatest contributions to living are small pleasures that can be seen each day, not the big bang events that happen here and there, usually no more frequent than a sighting of Halley's Comet.

Make it your business today to notice something beautiful, wholesome, and wondrous—stars in the heavens, a constellation like Orion, the Big Dipper, the Little Dipper, a sunrise, a sunset, stimulating music, a kind act by someone, an encouraging word from someone's lips.

5. Forget jumping over tall buildings in a single leap.

There are times in life when we wish we could be like Superman, but he is only a comic book character. It doesn't make any sense to try to act like him. No one has to conquer every weakness, solve every problem, or overcome each failure in a single day, but everyone can make a correction, change, or adjustment today by taking a step toward fulfilling his purpose for being on earth.

A big change is not necessarily required, either. It may be tiny, yet one about which at the end of the day, the person can say, "This I did to complete the reason I am still alive."

6. Let someone else determine whether life is worth continuing.

It would be smart for the decision maker to be someone who has demonstrated a broader perspective than what is naturally available to a human, someone who sees further and thinks deeper, someone who determined that each individual is worth a space in the place we call the world. Make it someone who has spared you from all the disasters that could have already come your way, and someone who has saved you from fatal accidents and other life-threatening calamities before now. Unless the choice is made by someone like that, the conclusions won't be as accurate and conclusive as they deserve to be.

LET DIVINE DETERMINATION BE
YOUR GUIDE!

7. Reconnect—I Belong Exercise/I Am Declaration.

Keep in mind that God's faith in the person who tried to end life has neither disappeared nor been rubbed out. More than anyone, anywhere, the Almighty still believes in the suicide survivor. How does a person like Derrick reconnect to such spiritual reality?

Others have found strength from the I Belong Exercise.

I

now

belong

to

God.

The exercise is never in past tense. It is not in future time. It is as current as today's weather.

If a person continues to have strong thoughts about bringing life to a close, return to these questions.

First question: "Where did my life originate?" Life did not come from your own hands. You did not dream it up. You could not will yourself into being and you were not in possession of anything required to pull it off. You had no say or input about your birth. The plain truth is, you had nothing to do with it—not a single anything!

Your life is the product of premeditated, carefully thought out, and unhurried divine intelligence of One who had what it took to be the Life-Giver. The breath of life came to you through His hands by the way of parents and preceding generations in your family. As eloquently stated by the apostle Paul: "We have come from the God who made the world and everything in it. Because of Him, we live and move and have our very being" (Acts 17:24, 28).

I AM DECLARATION

Then, you are here on a divine ticket. Any doubt tucked away in the back closet of your mind, probably forced on you by Adversity or Doubtful Worth, which causes you to think about ending life can be laid to rest. You have full authorization to write across your life in outlandishly bold letters the I Am Declaration:

I

am

from

GOD.

Say it. Again. **Shout it! LOUDER!**

Second question: "To whom or what does my life belong at this moment?" If a "what," it could be a possession. I have known people who ended their lives after their fortunes went down the drain. It is not difficult for meaning to lose its zip when a person is possessed by possessions. Things do not make good masters. Like devils, they want to take control and make the decisions. Possessions and destructive urges are the "what."

The most pertinent part in the question is: "To whom does my life belong this moment?" Lineage should determine ownership. Remember, you are from God. You belong to God. So, where would you get the right to take a life that you did not originate and that you do not own?

Third question: "How valuable is my life now?" Chemically, not much—a few dollars, other than vital organs. However, the value of a person's life is based on personhood comprised of all of the invisible stuff that makes us.

THE DIVINE STAKE IN A PERSON IS IMMEASURABLE!

If God thought enough to give you to the world and to accept you into His family, doesn't that make you a person of enormous value?

Fourth question: "Am I living in a way that complements my value as a person?" The previous question referred to character. This one emphasizes content. With the exception of a mental illness, anyone seriously considering ending his life has probably lost his sense of value. Therefore, he isn't living his value. As a result, he feels that his problems would be solved, if he were out of the picture. True, he would not have to face them, but he would create problems for others, in all likelihood those close and dear to him.

Survival Fact

Derrick felt that everyone would be better off if he were not around. I have known others who felt so overwhelmed that their will to live was like a cloud on a windy day, blown away.

This Survival Fact about the contents of a person's life is critical: Contents can be remodeled, removed, retired, and replaced. Since both character and content can change, there is hope. The help needed is not on the way—it is already available.

Where is Derrick now?

Today, Derrick is alive and well and no less interested in a better community and world, but this time, it's different. He has gained new perspective after times of rediscovery and restoration. Cynicism remains, but it isn't allowed to get the upper hand.

He hasn't become problem-free—no one has. But he keeps his problems in sharper, submissive focus.

Like dew after rain, imperfections still abound in the community and the world, but Derrick takes the approach everyone should: he does what he can do to improve things. He finds it much more rewarding to be the change he wants to see in the neighborhood and society, also in the family and church.

Derrick still struggles with his sense of value as a person, but he says, "I take it a day at a time." The I Belong Exercise and I Am Declaration continue to be his good friends. He has discovered truth in the words of Martin Luther King: "Faith is taking a step when you don't see the stairs."[56]

I almost hear God say, "I'm all for that."

Personal Survival Helps After a Loved One or Friend Ends His Life

An act of self-initiated death invariably sucks family members and friends into its impact area. In addition to shock and medical costs, feelings may include anger, guilt, and depression. Following the death of a child, one parent said, "It's like I killed myself."

1. Enter into a truce with the known.

Maybe the cause of suicide was obvious. Add the following to financial worries, suffering, mental illnesses, and serious physical problems I have already mentioned.

- Isolation
- Death of a relative or dear friend
- Unemployment
- Hopelessness
- Withering guilt feelings
- Alcohol or drug dependence
- Business reversal
- Severe, persistent problems at work
- Nagging family turmoil
- Shattered marriage
- Unwelcomed phase in life
- Overall despair with life

I have observed that an ongoing conflict with the cause drains strength, clarity of thought, emotional stamina, spiritual resources, and the will to move forward with life. Rather than a constant battle with the cause, center your prayers, attention, and efforts on the doable today.

2. Negotiate agreement with the unknown.

Self-inflicted death may have been a shocker. "I never would have thought it of her," someone said after the death of a friend. Oh, you may have known about problems—some could have involved you. But you didn't have the foggiest idea that the loved one or friend would take his own life.

There is much in life that is unknown. That's life. At best, our knowledge is limited. That's fact. Not knowing was no transgression. Lack of knowledge was no sin.

3. Squelch temptation to condemn and judge.

I see at least two compelling reasons to step away from condemnation and judgment. One, unless I have missed something in human experience and the scriptures, you and I are not the Almighty, so let's not try to act like it. Second, each of us has enough faults of our own to disqualify us. Jesus put it in words like these. "Let him who is perfect throw the first rock" (John 8:7). Condemnation and judgment are not becoming to a human being. If any is to be passed on, leave it to God. The Divine is best positioned for it.

4. Keep a tight grip on truth.

The loved one or friend could have been an upright member of the community, a good family person, well thought of by others, involved in the church, and a person of faith. Did the act of self-destruction remove him or her from God's love? Did suicide erase the presence of God from the loved one or friend? Worse yet, did it nullify his redeemed relationship with God and doom the person to everlasting damnation?

The answer is divorced from the act of self-destruction because the redeemed relationship doesn't depend on anything a human can do. Redemption is a positive response to the immensity, greatness, nature, purity, and offer of God and what He has done for everyone.

This Scripture has helped me: "Who or what has the power to separate us from the love of Christ? Does affliction? Hardship? Bad treatment by others? Hunger? Poverty? Danger? Demons from hell? Depression? Despair? Financial reverses? What others may do to us or say about us? Anything that happens today? Anything that could happen tomorrow? Death? Anything else we can possibly imagine? No, absolutely not! That which has the power to separate us from God's love in Jesus Christ hasn't been invented yet" (Rom. 8:35, 38).

Read these words often until you believe them and receive them as a personal assurance

5. Claim *your* life and future.

The death of the loved one or friend is real and final. There is no second chance for a makeover. A human life has ended, but it need *not* be the death of the survivors. Even if a chunk of you died with the loved one or friend, you can be resurrected. The future can be your friend.

Refuse to turn the future away. Start picking up the pieces that can be picked up. It's not time to quit living until God calls you into His heaven. If the loss is a spouse, there could be an unexpected surprise in the future as Randall and Eva discovered.

Randall was devastated when his wife took her own life. Some thought the cause was acute frustration with living. Eva's husband died before his time. The grief for both was deep and prolonged, yet not so permanent as to destroy them.

Make no mistake about it. Their grown children knew exactly what they were doing when they introduced Eva and Randall to each other. Although they were no frolicking spring chickens, the two found that fires of romance could be re-kindled.

They fell in love.

Randall proposed.

With all her heart, Eva replied, "Yes."

I performed the wedding ceremony.

When they were introduced as man and wife, their children clapped . . . for a long time. And an army of friends joined them. The couple has discovered a dimension of life grander than they felt possible.

"We had another chance," Eva said with a smile.
Randall didn't disagree.

A. P. S.
(Author's Postscript)

At some point in life, most people have suicidal thoughts, but we don't act on them. They are like a passing cloud—here for a moment, then gone, pushed out when common sense kicks in. Thankfully, causes for the thoughts are seen as temporary whereas death isn't.

According to the American Association of Suicidology, red flags should go up when a person threatens to kill himself, exhibits a strong death wish, makes his wish known, and looks for ways to make it happen.[57]

I have already mentioned loss of purpose and severe feelings of hopelessness as two of the forces behind it. The Association adds factors like extreme anxiety and agitation, inability to sleep or the tendency to sleep all the time, feeling trapped—"there's no way out for me," isolation from family, friends, and society, out-of-control anger—at times, rage, fanatical mood swings, and reckless involvement in risky behavior.[58]

Drug and alcohol abuse is another powerful ingredient. Results of an extensive examination of toxicology tests of those who took their own lives in thirteen states found that over 33 percent tested positive for alcohol, nearly 17 percent for opiates, 10 percent for cocaine, 8 percent for marijuana and 4 percent for amphetamines.[59]

Another core element is more critical than all the others. It is the absence of God awareness, a central contributor to loss of purpose and feelings of hopelessness.

"For me, it's as if God doesn't exist."
"God isn't watching out for me."
"God doesn't care."
"God isn't in control."
"God is not working for me."

From a practical standpoint, the impact of spiritual consciousness cannot be separated from all that makes up meaningful human experience any more than the fragrance from the rose.

Discussion Room

Agree	Disagree	
☐	☐	The suicide of a child predator is good riddance.
☐	☐	There is a time to live and a time to die.
☐	☐	Self-destruction is a mortal sin.
☐	☐	A mentally ill person who takes his own life isn't responsible.
☐	☐	The suicidal person got himself into his condition. He's the only one who can get himself out of it.
☐	☐	Everyone feels depressed occasionally.
☐	☐	Suicide among older persons is more understandable than among younger people.
☐	☐	Since most people who destroy themselves talk about it first, a compassionate listener will probably help them avoid actually doing it.
☐	☐	Most threats of suicide are ploys to get attention and should be disregarded.
☐	☐	Only the individual is responsible when he wants to take his own life.
☐	☐	It's okay for loved ones of those who take their own lives to be angry.
☐	☐	Suicide is a classic demonstration of selfishness.
☐	☐	The government has no business being involved in mental health.
☐	☐	Prayer can help a person who feels hopeless.
☐	☐	If E. J. had only trusted God, he wouldn't have destroyed himself.

What Do You Mean—Us?

Self-destruction is the ultimate display of individual determination. Nevertheless, family members, more-than-casual friends, church or faith-based services, and political leaders have important roles to play in the prevention and recovery process. They have the responsibility to form an Us Team.

Family

Since family members or friends are in closest contact with those who are struggling with life, they are in the most advantageous position to have a positive impact on them. The great challenge is to promote an environment of life.

- Take tell-tell signs seriously—like ones I have already outlined.
- Be an encourager—a person with a helpful word.
- Stay non-judgmental and free of condemnation. Self-destruction thrives on judgment and condemnation.
- Be an initiator. Nudge the one who exhibits suicidal tendencies to seek help.
- Be a pusher. More than an encourager and initiator, adamantly insist that the person participate in ways that could lead to recovery, but be sure to avoid belligerence.
- Be willing to talk about suicide and to listen.
- Be empathetic, not sympathetic—the person could use some understanding, but not agreement with reasons to justify self-initiated death.
- Be an ambassador of life, not death. Don't foster excuses to commit suicide
- Refrain from every temptation to remind a suicidal person of his faults and shortcomings; he reminds himself enough.
- Never dare the person to self-destruct; a dare lays down the gauntlet.
- As much as possible, remove every means that could be used to commit suicide.
- Find help—a counselor, minister, or a support group.

- Enlist in the People-Changer Corp. Volunteer to help start and conduct suicide education, prevention, and recovery services through your church.
- Be an advocate for public policies that remove conditions that help cause people to think about taking their lives (more under Political Leaders).

Church

Churches are called to be the mightiest hope for the hopeless, the strongest cathedral of restoration for the fallen, a brilliant light shining to all in need, a dependable lifeline without preconditions, and a welcome center inviting everyone to fulfill the higher purpose for which life has been given. Churches are in the most strategic position of any other group, organization, or governmental entity to lead sinners like each of us into the pure abundance of life.

- Promote an environment of acceptance. People who are thinking of suicide or have attempted it don't have leprosy and aren't untouchables.
- Discourage social and spiritual stigmas commonly attached to those who try to take their lives.
- Discard the Spiritual Midget Accusation often thrown at them. "You have little faith, no faith . . . shame, shame, shame!"
- Get serious about mobilizing a more responsible Rescue Mission: sermons, classes, and small groups.
- Present appropriate sermons once or twice a year. Ones that address the subject specifically, hopefully, thoughtfully, intelligently.
- Offer a class periodically. Four to six weeks in length won't wear down those who attend.
- At other times, organize a small group. It offers prime opportunity for discussion and support.
- Don't forget a Recovery Group especially for those who have attempted to take their lives, as well as family members or friends—8–10 weeks to start has worked effectively.

- Faith-based and professional Counseling Services. A small congregation can team with a larger church or several small churches. Some have successfully joined an established service.
- Publicize sermons, classes, groups, and services to the community. Get as many to attend and become as involved as possible. You won't help them if you don't reach them.
- Clear the air. The church fulfils its seek-and-save mission best by being a hospital where people in need go for healing, not a sanctuary reserved exclusively for saints to rest.

Political Leaders

In the last several decades, government has awakened to responsibilities in causes of mental health. The amount of funds allocated on all levels from City Councils to federal departments is now in the hundreds of millions of dollars annually. Many communities have mental health programs, crisis intervention centers, and prevention networks. The commitment is commendable, but government is not the answer. *It is an agent.*

The order of responsibility is:

Individual—there is no substitute for personal initiative and responsibility.
Family—the most genuine core of social security.
Church—faith-centered compassionate care.
Government—service with and by, then for people, keeping focus on the common good.

"For people" is third in my order of priorities under government services. Doing for people is demeaning, dehumanizing, and detrimental to those who can do for themselves. At least, what they can partly do for themselves.

Many government programs address symptoms more than causes. The greatest good for the most people will be achieved when more attention is directed to the causes of problems. What are some causes that may contribute to suicides?

- Discrimination—treatment as second-class citizens, or worse
- Denied opportunity—closed doors to advancement
- Inferior educational services—lack of access to the best programs
- Injustices—unequal treatment based on superficial reasons
- All other social impairments that depress individual initiative

You have noticed that everything I have outlined is a matter over which the person who suffers has no direct control. Each is imposed on the person and contributes to his or her feelings of despair about life. I hope you also noticed that nothing relieves the individual of personal responsibility, a basic tenet of the healthful and wholesome life.

Government has the power to better address problems like these by creating *polices* and *environment* that promote solutions. Political leaders would serve the best interests of everyone by revisiting the issues, rethinking involvement, and enthusiastically implementing new ways to solve problems. Politicians respond to pressures. Family members, churches, and others in communities have the power to exert pressure in a persuasive, yet nonbelligerent way.

Prayer for Hope

God of mercy, help those who are bedeviled by thoughts of taking their lives to believe that it is unnecessary. Provide a way for them to be aware that they are accepted as Your loved children and grant strength to overcome fears and feelings of worthlessness which entomb them.

Trusting Your presence, triumphant Lord, may they be held up by hope. By Your grace, embolden them to become new persons. Bless with an assurance that their remaining days can be full of promise and service.

Rescue them from destroying their tomorrows and give them renewed reason for living. In the name of the redeeming One who offers life which overcomes urges of self-destruction. Amen.

Good News

Have mercy on me, Lord. I want to die. My insides are in agony and my soul is very troubled. How long, God, how long must I be tormented? My will to live has disappeared . . . The strength you need must come from the Lord's mighty power (Ps. 6:2–3; Eph. 6:10).

Chapter Ten

Embarrassment. Humiliation.
Shame—if word leaked out.

Nelson, Respectable Person—Except to Family Members

According to sources at Mayo Clinic, millions in America suffer abuse at the hands of family members every year.[60] It didn't catch me off guard because I have seen such behavior before and in the most unexpected places. Still, I was perplexed by Nelson who hurt those closest to him.

Considered upstanding and socially acceptable, he would not entertain the thought of behaving outside the four walls of his house the way he sometimes did behind closed doors. Nelson was successful and a believer, yet acted like a failure and pagan when he verbally, emotionally, and spiritually abused his wife and children.

Samuel Butler, the English composer and novelist, said that people do not stumble over mountains, but over molehills.[61] Nelson was a walking example. Not much was required to send him into a tirade, like the time he got lost while going to visit friends. When someone suggested that he stop and ask directions, he yelled, "Shut up! When I need your help, I'll ask for it!"

Disagreements and slower than instant obedience of family members were signs of what he judged to be weaknesses—no, not much was necessary. So when a son came home with a C on his report card, you'd thought Armageddon had come. And it continued in one way or another for several days.

Abuse has many faces—physical, sexual, emotional, and verbal. Later I mention one more—spiritual.

Seven Guidebook Answers— Let the Sunshine In

1. Feel the shock of it.

Every abusive person would do himself/herself a favor by putting each type of abuse in the same bag instead of neatly categorizing one as worse than another. For instance, many people think, "What I say isn't as bad as punching the person in the nose." I remember the grade school rhyme repeated during little schoolyard squabbles: "Sticks and stones may break my bones, but words can never hurt me." In human experience, this isn't true, according to Patricia Evans, author of The Verbally Abusive Relationship.[62]

Cruel words can inflict more damage than broken bones. Cruel words crush the spirit, poke holes in personal confidence, and make a person physically sick. A youngster whose father constantly leveled criticisms at him, developed stomach and digestive problems that physicians determined were caused by the father's abuse. Sure enough, when the abuse stopped, the boy began to improve. Within a year, he was the picture of vibrant health.

They may be subtle and cagey, nonetheless, emotional and verbal abuse are as real and serious as physical violence, and possibly more catastrophic. Since there are no cracked ribs and black eyes, they may not be thought to be as horrific, but the scars they leave can be deeper and longer lasting.

EVERY COLOR OF ABUSE IS EQUALLY UGLY!

Abuse often begins without a lot of fanfare—little digs and sly criticism—before moving on to hurtful, cutting comments. Progressively, outbursts and controlling behavior jump on the steamroller as the abuse becomes more frequent and severe. On the other hand, the abuse may remain low key and still possess all the destructive force of thunderous incidents.

In my experience, the people who have been cured are those who went through a shock step.

2. Knock it off.

I am talking about Place Fault Elsewhere Games that are the sport of choice among abusers. What are some of the favorites?

- Existing Environment—"Pressures, stress, and tension I'm under are responsible."
- It's Beyond Me Affliction—"She/he provoked me."
- Early Example—"Daddy Joe or Mama Jane or Grandpa Charlie or Uncle Ed or Aunt Susie did it. I learned from them."
- Extraterrestrial Enforcer—In the words of comedian Flip Wilson, "The devil made me do it."
- Elusive Energy—"Under the circumstances, I can't help myself."

What if there is no more than a tiny grain of truth in games like these? That is still enough to make them a pathetic litany of escapism so that responsibility can be placed away from the abuser. These games sneer at facts on the ground and form an evil immaculate deception.

3. Sock it to oneself.

A tougher assessment of damages caused by abuse is in order because they are severe on members of the family, both the ones on whom abuse is inflicted and those who are within its environment. The abuser doesn't get off unscathed either. For example:

Disrespect—any victim in his/her right mind cannot possibly admire an abusive person. Admiration is earned. Even if other deserving characteristics are demonstrated, abusive behavior throws a blanket over them. A teenage son expressed it by saying, "The way he (father) acted drowned out some good things in his life."

Decreased Self-Respect—in the silent hall alone with himself, an abuser tends to think less of him or herself. Ten minutes after an outburst, how should he/she feel? What about an hour after the fireworks?

Weakened Self—Most abusive persons I have known felt they were unable to keep from doing it. Actually, in the emotional and spiritual condition that had the upper hand at the time, they were weak, but not incurably so.

Diminished Sense of Self-Esteem—"For me to do something like this, I must be a low body, a nobody." Yes, she acted like it, but she wasn't.

Doubts about Purpose—"Is this included in the life for which I was created?" Unless action is taken which says, "No, it is not," the lid on a fuller life will not open any further than it is.

Guilt Feelings—After repeated episodes, a man said, "I was so ashamed . . . humiliated." In some cases, guilt has useful purposes. This is one of those times.

Fear of Exposure—"What if people at work or church or business associates found out?" Whatever esteem these people have for the abuser would be splintered. Under their breath, they would probably say, "What a pity. I would not have thought that of him/her."

Severance or Interruption of Emotional Bonds with the Victim—The positive bond that is needed to connect people to each other is cut or at least suspended. Referring to her mother, a daughter confirmed it when she said, "I don't want to be around her. I can't stand her."

Conflict in Family Life—In the basic unit in society, abusive behavior is a specialist at causing chaos. Where there is chaos, anxiety and stress come as natural as destruction follows the hurricane.

Parting of the Ways—Abusers shouldn't be all that surprised when victims move to separate themselves from them. It probably should have happened when it became apparent that any commitment to changing was on par with the likelihood of winning a $500 million lottery. Parting of the ways for dependent children may be delayed for a few years, but it is not likely to be denied.

If an abusive person will consider how utterly ridiculous it is to go into tirades, if he/ she will think of how uncouth and ignorant it makes him/her look, and if the person would imagine all the defeated people on every continent of the world with whom he/she becomes one—it should be more than enough for that person to declare open warfare on abusive behavior.

4. Employ the tick-tock strategy.

The next time circumstances begin to ripen for an outburst, an abuser who puts time on his or her side takes a step toward a personal sunshine.

Immediately take a breather. Put a lock on your lips and walk away for a moment, a few minutes, even longer. Time out provides opportunity to collect your feelings, stem the slide into an explosion, and marshal your inner resources to further deal with forces sucking you toward an outburst.

5. Lock it in.

During time out, sit down, close your eyes, and focus on a peaceful thought as a substitute for an agitating thought. It could be a calming incident while on the job or with a friend, a tranquil scene, a beautiful flower. Then put peaceful words to the peaceful thought. Give voice to the thought. Say it. Words solidify and inject reality into thoughts.

6. Surround yourself with a flock.

There is help for anger management and re-direction of impulses so that you can more effectively deal with an inner disorder that should not have been allowed to last as long as it has. No matter how determined and noble your intentions, a Lone Ranger effort will not get you through to wholeness.

It takes a flock, people who offer encouragement, support, correction, counsel, love (maybe, ultra tough love), and prayers. Connect with a group made up of people who are working at overcoming the same problem. A family of faith should be a supportive group. An accepting group like that can be a silent sentinel of positive reinforcement and acceptance, not of the abuse, but of the abuse-free person he can become.

Abusive persons, especially men, have shared how critical it was for them to stop being pigheaded at the idea of professional counseling. One said, "I thought it would be a sign of weakness." Another added, "I felt I could lick my problem without that kind of help."

A carefully chosen counselor could be an angel bringing the newness that awaits an abuser. Faith-based professionals are ready to be of assistance.

7. Build on rock.

There is a Dominance Dispute that needs to be settled. A much better follower of Jesus than me knew what it was all about. Paul said, "I can promise to do what is right, then cannot do it . . . I don't understand my own actions; when I want to act the way I know is right, I act the very way I despise . . . Evil lurks close by. It makes me feel wretched—who will deliver me?" (Rom. 7:15–24).

The dominance issue is not primarily between the abusive person and those who are abused. It is *within* the abuser.

PITIFUL SELF VERSUS POWERED SELF

The skirmish—one woman called it a "raging battle"—is between Pitiful Self that succumbs to impulses leading to outbursts and Powered Self that confronts and handles those impulses. The outcome depends on which self is permitted to dominate.

Displays of destructive impulses hold an abuser in captivity. By coping and conquering, the curtain can be lowered and closed on a reign of negative behavior.

The Powered Self opens the door.

Just ask Nelson.

On a deeper level, Nelson discovered the desire, will, and strength that are available from God and dispensed to seeking, trusting people—discoveries, combined with other game changing factors like "flock" and professional help. That brings some closure to the Dominance Dispute.

The incomparable Michelangelo explained one of his sculptures, "I saw the angel in the marble and carved until I set him free."[63] The discoveries I mentioned worked together to help Nelson envision freedom from abusive behavior and launch his journey out of bondage.

Coping and conquering still go on, but the curtain edges closer toward closing.

God likes that.

His family does, too!

A. P. S.
(Author's Postscript)

Nelson's family was thrilled and thankful for the change in his behavior, but the children will need to take special care when they are adults. There are two roads they can take. One is to avoid becoming an abusive person in the same vein as Nelson was before changing. I know of children who have been so repulsed by a parent's negative behavior that they insisted, "I will never be like that."

The other road is to fall into the same vicious trap as the parent and become abusive. Even some who have sworn to avoid it find themselves following in dear old dad's or mom's footsteps. What is the reason?

Social science has clearly demonstrated the persuasiveness of example on thinking, attitude, and lifestyle. "Like father, like son" is one way of looking at it; also a "chip off the old block" and the "apple doesn't fall far from the tree" are common sayings. It is the undeniable influence of instruction by observation. Not a single word has to be spoken.

Long before our day of sophisticated science and psychology of human behavior, the Hebrews were faced with the reality of "sins of the fathers." The third of Ten Commandments given thousands of years ago mentioned the sins of the fathers (parents) affecting children to the third and fourth generations (Ex. 20:5). And again, children in regards to admission of sins—their own—and sins of their fathers (Lev. 26:39–40).

However, molds are made to be broken. Someone reared in an abusive family does *not* have to become an abuser. The behavior of a family member does *not* give anyone a free pass to similar behavior. The power of negative example will crumble before the awesome power of positive behavior!

Spiritual Abuse

What about spiritual abuse? Fanatical Islam, cults, and other systems of religions that enforce off-the-chart requirements and ungodly behavior are cases in point, but they aren't the reason I brought up the subject. Well meaning believers in Christ are also abusive when they insist that everyone interpret the scriptures for faith and life exactly as they do, that those who don't are terribly wrong, and that if others were as spiritual as themselves, they would follow the same paths.

Don't get me wrong. First-level essentials of faith are non-negotiable. For instance, God the Father Almighty, maker of heaven and earth, and Jesus Christ, God's Son . . . crucified . . . raised from the dead . . . direct and personal relationship with the Lord by grace (undeserved favor) through faith.

Beyond first-level essentials, not everyone has to hold my views, and it isn't necessary for me to agree with everyone else. Spiritual life isn't at risk for either of us. Heaven isn't on the line either.

Discussion Room

Agree	Disagree	
☐	☐	It's better to blow out (get feelings out) than to blow up (keep feelings pent-up inside).
☐	☐	The psychological, emotional make-up of some people makes it impossible for them to control their impulses.
☐	☐	As long as an abusive person asks forgiveness, his behavior is okay.
☐	☐	Everyone is called on to put up with something he doesn't like in other people.

Agree	Disagree	
☐	☐	When an abusive person won't change, it's okay to leave . . .
☐	☐	To divorce . . .
☐	☐	Not okay to leave . . .
☐	☐	Or to divorce.
☐	☐	Physical abuse is the worst kind.
☐	☐	An abusive person will never fully get over his behavior. It will always cast a shadow over his life.
☐	☐	Any way you look at it, abusers like Nelson are disgusting.
☐	☐	Family members need to be more careful that they do not give an abusive person any excuse to act abusively.
☐	☐	Agreement on and adherence to more than first-level essentials are necessary in a church for there to be harmony and teamwork required to accomplish the mission entrusted to the church.
☐	☐	When it comes to religious beliefs in the family and church, it would be better to "live and let live."
☐	☐	Any person can change, if he really wants to change.
☐	☐	My church has more important things to do than deal with abuse.
☐	☐	It is important to love an abusive person in spite of his negative behavior.

Some Abusive People I've Known

- The Boss—compulsion to control others to the extent of unilaterally determining menu, activities, places to go, dress, and finances. Example: A husband convinced his wife, a successful banker, that she might know how to handle money on the job, but not in the home.
- Slama-Jama Authority—slams others by name calling, put downs publicly and privately, hurling insults, and making the abused feel bad about oneself.
- Dandy Denier—denies that behavior is abuse. "It's no big deal."
- All Wise Potentate—doesn't ask, seek, find, or welcome opinions and input of family members.
- Great Decision Maker—single-handedly makes everyday decisions affecting others.
- Isolation Specialist—insists on separation of the abused from friends and independent, personal interests.
- Mighty Enforcer—attempts to impose his/her will and way on the abused, including sexually, when it isn't welcomed.
- Suspicious One—doesn't trust the abused.

A Little Honesty . . . Good for the Soul— Also Relationships and Life!

Abuse is more about power and control than anger.

It is not primarily about the abused.

It shows up personality glitches such as narcissism, anti-social tendencies, and inner conflict that struggle in an effort to cope with self and life.

Steps to protect those subject to verbal and emotional abuse—including family members—are as important as protection from physical abuse.

Abuse is a pattern of behavior stemming from a combination of emotional and spiritual anemia.

Behavior can change—emotional and spiritual anemia can be cured.

Prayer to See the Light

Providing Lord, strength to tame outbursts, guidance to ways by which to avoid the kind of confrontations that invite wild responses, and good sense to alter behavior are all available. Inner rejuvenation needed to step over, go around, or tunnel under the temptation to berate others is possible. Practical help to deal with feelings is within reach. An enriched understanding of oneself is within Your will. People can come to You for an extreme spiritual make-over.

Grant seeking and receiving mercies to those in need.

Come to family members with power to discover the determination to do everything within their power to bring it to an end. Provide courage to take steps to remove themselves, and those for whom they are responsible, from the environment. Bless them with others who care and will help deal with bruised attitudes, battered personalities, and secret self-doubts.

Oh God, may they again feel the unrestricted love in which You hold them and believe that they can rise from their experiences to live with purpose. Grant another opportunity to live in the joyous freedom for which they were created. In the spirit of the One who sets people free. Amen.

Good News

Incline your ear and come to me; listen so that you may live . . . The Lord in you is greater than the evil one (Isa. 55:3; 1 John 4:4).

---

Chapter Eleven

*"Has she lost her mind—
what did we do wrong?"*

Elaine, Child of Believers (and God)— Lost in a Wilderness

I remember the television commercial with the line, "Whatever life brings, bring it on." Sometimes life brings dreadful disappointments.

Relationships fracture. Love strays. Dreams evaporate. Ambitions are thwarted. Aims are intercepted. Success is denied. A business fails. Promotions are rejected. The company downsizes. Still worse, it relocates. An economic downturn leads to job loss. The door to a sought-after opportunity closes. There is a sudden calamity. A neighbor loses the ability to make sensible decisions. Friends drift away. Loved ones die young. Others have unthinkable diseases.

Children and grandchildren wander into a personal wilderness.

It happened to Elaine.

She was a beautiful child and welcomed as a gift into the family. Through parental example, Elaine's young years were blessed. She was taught the way she should live. As a teenager, Elaine lived trust in the Lord and was joyful about involvement in the church, extra-curricular activities at school, and community projects to benefit the less advantaged. She entered college with enough enthusiasm to make great dreams come true.

Then there was a disastrous turn in her life. An absence from faith, dropout from community activities, and loss of interest in the university were obvious to all who knew her. Close friends from years past were put on the sidelines. Elaine began to claim people as friends who demonstrated that they weren't friends at all.

Disrespect for parents, denial of ways in which she was reared, behavior that repudiated values, and forsaken dreams came over Elaine like a tornado swoops down in America's Mississippi Valley.

It was a crushing blow to her parents, Tim and Sarah, and grandparents, Marjorie and Walter. They felt like the mother whose child left in Henry Clay Work's ship that never returned.

Having children who go astray is nothing new. Now, though, there seems to be more ways enticing them to detour into a Land of Left Out. When it happens, the hurt felt by devoted parents and grandparents has few comparisons.

"Has my child lost his mind?" "How could this happen to our child?" "Is everything we've tried to do gone down the drain?" "Is the detour permanent?" "What did we do wrong?"

Is everything lost?

Did they fail?

Guidebook Answers—Ten Step Wilderness Survival Program

1. Review reasons for going astray.

This helps satisfy questions that family and friends have and explain the wandering phenomenon. Don't be surprised to find that reasons include:

Misguided desire—"I want to do it."
Misjudged evaluation—"It looked like it would be more fun."
Misplaced love—"My boyfriend/girlfriend led me there."
Curiosity—"I think it's important to see what else there is to life."
Experimentation—"I just want to try something different."
Perceived need—"I felt it was necessary for my life experience."
Excitement—"I'm searching for more zip in my life."
Independence—"I have a right to a life on my terms."

Rite of passage—"Everyone sows their wild oats."

Drug use may also be a factor, especially marijuana which some consider to be merely recreational and harmless. But not according to Dr. Marc Galanter, one of America's most authoritative voices about drug use.

> Pot changes the developing brain . . . chronic use (of it) can affect certain centers in the brain that control emotion and reason. Research shows that regular use may also lead to mental health problems. Youth who use marijuana weekly have double the risk of depression later in life, and are three times more likely than non-users to have suicidal thoughts.[64]

A physician friend has witnessed the trail of drug use beginning with marijuana. "Hardly ever does it stop there." He explained that use of it might start as early as in childhood, accelerate in adolescence, and spread into use of other drugs.

Do not expect to find reasons like these for taking a drastic detour in life: "I believe it is the right thing to do" or "I don't see anything wrong with it." These indicate that a child probably has not lost his mind, that family did nothing so wrong as to bring it on, and that not everything parents endeavored to do has been wiped out.

But there is another explanation—the rabble-rousing rebel within.

A child, and every human being, has a streak of rebellion inside. It is accompanied by an inclination to do wrong which makes itself at home inside each one and shows its countless faces in human activity. A good word for the manifestation of the rebel is "sin." Everyone is prone to sin. A very devoted person put it this way: "I am a sinner, an unclean man" (Isa. 6:5).

2. Replenish down times.

There are periods in life when people feel like they have been turned off. Sarah described it like being a nomad in a desert that stretches as far as the eye can see.

Points of Life are good for times like that.

For example, "God gave me life. God gave life to my child."

"God still claims me as His child. God still claims my child as His child."

"God is still for me. God is still for my child."

"God is still with me. My child is still within the sphere of God's presence."

"God provides me strength. God's strength is still available to my child."

"My purpose in life is still good. My child's purpose in life still remains good."

"I will not be destroyed by the wilderness, and I refuse to let the wilderness destroy my child."

3. Replay bright moments.

In my own life, I came to the conclusion that there are Front Door Blessings and Side Door Blessings. Front Door favors are more obvious because they include family, friends, funds, food, shelter, and clothes. Side Door favors are ones that aren't as noticeable, yet, just as real such as: bad things which could have happened but didn't; accidents, illnesses, and adversities that could have been much worse but weren't; problems that looked, then turned away; and failure that could have been catastrophic but wasn't.

Occasionally, think of a moment of unexpected blessing in the child's life, a blessing enjoyed by child and parents together, an incident when the child could have been killed or injured and was spared, a family fun time, and a trying experience which was handled successfully.

Replaying bright moments help reinforce determination to deny success to the demons at work in a child's life.

4. Reestablish manageable perspective.

It is human nature to see goings-on through a magnifying lens. The way they appear is not necessarily the way they are. As a result, they are blown beyond the proportions they deserve.

A child in the wilderness is serious. Make no mistake about it. Yet, it is probably not as bad as it could be. There are worse things that could happen.

Do not permanently lose perspective and you will be better equipped as a parent to handle the realities of wilderness events.

5. Reinstate a more complete picture.

Life is like a book. This one, like all others, is written one page at a time. Each day is a page in the book of life and only one page of a person's life is written in a day—successes, failures, and ways of behavior, thinking, and talking.

In some cases, a life page once written can be re-written. If not, a subsequent page can be written which changes the dynamics of one that is not rewrite-able.

The back country through which a person goes should not be considered the last page in the final chapter of that person's life. It is a temporary detour. Agree and believe that it is.

6. Reminder—unconditional love.

A couple whose child was in a remote wilderness in life reminded him occasionally, "There is nothing you can say or do that will stop us from loving you." At times, they admitted, they had to force the words out.

A wayward child may move heaven and earth trying to get a parent or other family members to quit. Most parents I know with children who have journeyed into a personal wilderness have gone through periods when they felt like unloving the children and, if they had exercised their druthers, would have finalized a total declaration of independence from the children.

Let children know that love for them is firm, in spite of themselves.

Love like that is unconditional, but accountability is not.

7. Reject the tendency to do for.

The Accountability Commandment insists, "Thou shalt not do for a family member what the family member can and should do for himself."

Parents must take responsibility for anything they do or fail to do that helps a child stay in the wilderness a second longer than the child would on his own. The child is accountable for continuing to pursue a losing lifestyle.

I have seen good results when supply lines that make it possible for a child to sidestep responsibility are shut off including money, transportation, cell phone, other subsidies, and comforts which would be enjoyed if he were living on the positive side of life.

By shutting off the spigot, parents may help the child to feel so miserable with wanderings that he will want to bid it goodbye sooner. Otherwise parents may lead the child to develop a system of family welfare. "You're my parents, for goodness sake, you owe me support."

There are children who have eloquently argued that they are entitled to it. A misguided one claimed that financial support is a responsibility of parents for life—from the cradle to the grave. "You brought us into the world, so you take care of us for as long as we are in the world."

Any parent who falls for it, or any shadow of it, leads the child to an obnoxious condition—a do-nothing, be-nothing life.

8. Refuse the herky-jerky merry-go-round.

This is a cousin to rejecting the tendency to do for a child what the child can do for himself. Respond to their contacts, but there is no reason to rush it. At least, not every time. Avoid jumping at calls like an indentured servant. Make the child wait a bit once in awhile.

Deliberate delay may cause a child to think that parents actually do have interests other than the child.

You do, don't you?

Refusal to be jerked around could hasten their return to the high road.

9. Remember in prayer.

I suggest prayers similar to this one: *Thank You, God for still loving _____ and for keeping in place the purpose for which You gave _____ life. I ask You to protect _____ and spare him/her from doing anything which would permanently scar his/her life. Cause something to happen which will point to a new beginning and grant the strength needed to break the demonic forces that would enslave and destroy _____ permanently. Amen.*

I want to emphasize once more the importance of being person- and petition-specific in prayers. Effects of prayers may not be noticeable instantly. If results are not visible at the moment and there is a tendency to be unsettled about it, consider how much worse off the person could be if no prayers were offered.

10. Recommit to Covenant Connection.

In daily affairs, a covenant is an agreement between two parties in which each one makes specific promises. For instance, I live in a covenant community. The association representing the homeowners made promises to one another, and these are outlined in the covenant.

But the Covenant Connection I am referring to here is a spiritual agreement between God and His people based on a relationship established through commitment by the parties to the covenant. The parties are God and those who trust in Him.

According to my understanding, the covenant with believing people is that God will be their God forever, at all times, in all places, and through every conceivable circumstance (the inconceivable ones, too). The personal application is this: "I belong to God for as long as God lives."

I have seen the Covenant Connection get a parent or grandparent from where he is—the nightmare of a child who has strayed far away—to where the parent or grandparent could be, a God-held person who can deal with experiences brought on by a wandering child. The Covenant Connection provides a tenacious covering that strengthens the faith that triumph will come. There is more.

This Covenant Connection also has dynamic implications through believing parents to children and grandchildren. In this regard, the covenant assures that the God of believing parents is and will also be the God of their children. It is traced to Abraham in ancient times: "I (your God) will establish my covenant as an everlasting covenant between me and you and your descendants after you for the generations to come, to be your God and the God of your descendants after you" (Gen. 17:7, NIV). The catalyst for this covenant was faith—Abraham's. The seal of this covenant was faithfulness—God's (Gen. 15:6).

As with most things which pack a spiritual wallop, the covenant involved practical expressions in everyday life. For example, "Rear a child in the way he should live and when he is old, he will not turn from it" (Prov. 22:6). The sign of this covenant in those times was circumcision of male children.

As I see it, the Covenant continued with the coming of Jesus and applies to believers this very day. The catalyst is still faith and the seal is still faithfulness, but the sign for followers of Jesus became baptism. The idea was conveyed through these words: "The promise is for you and your children and for all who are far off" (Acts 2:39, NIV).

An expression in daily life still includes, "Rear your child in the way he should live and, even if he departs from what you have taught, he will return to it at some time in his life."

As a sign of the Covenant Connection, some followers of Christ have children baptized at a very young age. Others have children publicly dedicated or engage in some other visible response of faith that acknowledges that children of believers uniquely belong to God. By word and deed, some have reared their children in the way they should live. None of them should let a child's detour into the wilderness yank the promise of the covenant from under their spiritual feet.

Believe that the child will return from a far country sooner or later, even if it is not in the parent's lifetime.

Depend on God's faithfulness (reliability). Make it a spiritual guarantee on a divine level.

Ask and believe that it will be sooner. If the awaited return from the wilderness is not sooner, count on God to pull it off at sometime. It is never advantageous to equate divine delay with divine denial.

But what about parents like Bonnie and Franklin? "We have a straying child. We are Christians, but our spiritual family doesn't baptize, dedicate, or perform another public faith exercise for children. What about my child?"

And the Marshalls who lamented, "We weren't believers during our child's growing up years, so we did none of those baptism, dedication things. And we didn't particularly rear our child in the way he should live. Are we now on the outside looking in?"

Also the father who confessed that when their child was younger, they were, at best, "casual" believers. "We didn't give any thought to a Covenant idea."

State of As-Is Faith

No one needs to think he has to come up a mile behind and a dollar short. Everyone can lift up his eyes, take heart, and exercise the State of As-Is Faith based on this spiritual promise. "Believe on the Lord, Jesus Christ, and you will be delivered (saved), you AND your family" (Acts 16:31). To me, it means:

a. God's love that was embodied in Jesus Christ is equal for everyone. It is no less for one than for any other one. This means that all parents and children are loved—*completely, perfectly*!

b. Trust yourself as you are and where you are—as much as you know how to—to God's goodness, mercy and grace. No one can do more. No one should do less.

c. Promptly follow-up by pledging children, whatever their ages and condition and wherever they are, to the same merciful God. "Lord, I dedicate (name) to You and ask that _____ be brought to trust in You and to the way out of his wilderness. By Your mercy, I claim _____ for Your forgiven family. Amen."

d. Engage now whatever faith is at your disposal to live like the child of God you are. The quantity, a lot vs. a little, is not the issue, but fullness is—all you have, as much as you know.

Divine Force of Will Not

Receive the power from God and act on it to commission the Divine Force of Will Not. No matter how depraved the wild country or how far a child roams, refuse to surrender the child to the devils of darkness. Insist time and again, "I will *not* let demons of the wilderness have him, so help me God!"

There is an exit door out of the wilderness.

There is life for the parents and the child on the other side.

What about Tim, Sarah, Marjorie and Walter?

"We staved off being victimized by Elaine's wilderness," according to Sarah, "and losing our sanity." Walter added that he found new meaning from the idea of a Covenant Connection. "We had given lip service to it for years. But the truth is, we didn't understand it. In Elaine's wilderness, it became a fresh stimulus to our faith."

And Elaine?

The road out was not an overnight sensation, but she started on the way. She is still on it. I've heard that there is nothing wrong with younger persons that twenty-five years or so will not cure.

In the case of parents and grandparents of people like Elaine, there is nothing that God cannot cure.

Or will not.

That produces some cheers amid the tears, doesn't it?

A. P. S.
(Author's Postscript)

The well-loved poet, Ella Wheeler Wilcox, wrote,

> The only folk who give us pain
> Are those we love the best.[65]

It reminds me that authentic love avoids a scorched earth treatment of children by looking for responsible ways to keep the road to recovered relationship open. Hatefulness and, in more cases than not, disownership burns bridges. Accountability doesn't.

Holding a child accountable prepares the road to recovery and establishes the map by which to travel that road. I referred to supply lines a few paragraphs ago. Let me reemphasize—discontinuation of supply lines does *not* arbitrarily burn bridges. A meandering child may try to convince parents that it does. That is a maneuver as old as the species—don't fall for it.

Another thing about this love—it does not require that you relinquish your moral and spiritual principles. In fact, surrendering them could delay, even damage, recovery for the family member. The last thing the wanderer needs during a wilderness journey is a parent or grandparent who tosses principles aside like socks with holes in them.

I have observed helpful results from principles that include conditions for living in the family house. To me, they are also known as staying-at-home-privileges. Conditions need to be lovingly and firmly made clear in a collected, controlled setting. Even then, don't be surprised when bombarded by accusations like, "Now you're trying to run my life. I'll do with it as I please."

Accept—Abide or Reject—Eject

Remember accountability? Squeeze it tightly. Stay steady against intimidation.

Parents are the ones to set ground rules for living in the home. A child has yet to earn that right. Besides, children have a choice—accept and abide or reject and eject. If the choice is to reject, always keep the welcome light on.

When parents see a wayward child, a hug speaks a language that needs no interpreter.

Discussion Room

Agree	Disagree	
☐	☐	If Sarah, Tim, Marjorie and Walter had been more alert, they would have kept Elaine out of the wilderness.
☐	☐	Parents can be too domineering.
☐	☐	Grandparents aren't first responders when there are problem grandchildren.
☐	☐	During and after adolescence, peers influence people more than family.
☐	☐	People at church need to be more supportive of families having problems.
☐	☐	The idea of "accept and abide or reject and eject" is too extreme.
☐	☐	Erring children deserve old-fashioned tongue lashings.

Agree	Disagree	
☐	☐	The Covenant Connection doesn't square with reality.
☐	☐	Parents should keep hands off of wayward children and let whatever happens, happen.
☐	☐	If parents reared children the way people use to, the children wouldn't go astray.
☐	☐	Society has a major influence on individual behavior.
☐	☐	Elaine's problem was nothing more than a spiritual deficiency.
☐	☐	God is ready, willing, and able to come with help to people with problems.

Twelve Game Changers on the Return Road from a Personal Wilderness—from Some Who Traveled It

Sickness—"I became sick of the wilderness, and the wilderness made me sick. After six years, my body is still recovering."

Better alternative—"After several brushes with death, I thought anything would be preferable to some experiences I went through."

Bottom out—"I had to sink as far as I could, and did."

Serious about changing—"More than think about it, hope for it, wish for it, or talk about it, I had to do it (work at returning from waywardness)."

Definite commitment to change—"Half-hearted stabs didn't cut it."

Support—"Somebody who believed in me made more difference than I can explain."

A lifeline—"My family threw several my way before I grabbed one."

Enabler-free—"Family members and old friends who wanted to be helpful had to quit making my rebellion easier."

Opportunity—"I was given the chance to do better immediately (school and work)."

Community—"It was made clear many times that I didn't have to face my need alone, and, as I found out, I didn't."

Reinforcement—"Firm reminders that I wasn't put on earth for the kind of life I was living meant more than I've ever told those who said it."

Faith—"I honestly feel that I would still be in it (personal far country) if it had not been for God's intervention and the prayers of others who thought I was important."

Prayer for Return

Faithful Redeemer, come to those in a personal wilderness with disenchantment for the way they are now. Burn within them a desire to leave the back country in favor of life with purpose. Help them to see the road out of their wanderings. Do something to them and through others on their behalf that turns their eyes toward tomorrows full of hope and service.

Parents and grandparents also need Your help, Lord. When they are bewildered, direct their thoughts to Your greatness. When blinded by waywardness of children, visit them with an awareness that You are close by. When agitated, come with a calmness that has stilled the lives of others who have gone through similar experiences.

Bless them, gracious God, with wisdom to say and strength to do what could make a difference. Be through them voices of responsibility, determination, encouragement, higher expectations, correction, and motivation that push children to reach for their stars. Keep hope alive in them. In the grace of Him who makes it possible for people to change courses in life. Amen.

Good News

The Lord says, "I will come to you and fulfill my gracious promise to bring you back from this place" (Jer. 29:10).

Chapter Twelve

Prosperous, yet, a pauper.

M. T., Prescription Addiction—Little Pills, Large Problems

A television commercial shows a dejected dope dealer standing on a half lighted street corner puffing on his cigarette like a steam powered locomotive straining to reach the top of a steep incline. All the while, he complains, "I've lost my customers. I've lost them to the pills they find in their parents' medicine cabinets at home."

Methamphetamine, cocaine, heroin, and the rest in the arsenal of illegal drugs have had to make room for the new kid on the block—abuse through misuse and overuse of physician prescribed medications.

According to the U. S. Department of Health & Human Services, there are more than 20 million illicit drug users, 11 million abusers of alcoholic beverages, 71 million tobacco users (those in the age 18–25 group account for 41 percent of them), and 36 million nicotine dependent persons. Children and adolescents make up nearly 10 percent of the problem.[66]

Similar statistics for PDA (prescription drug abuse) aren't available as yet, but there is enough information known to identify it as an alarming trend that is accelerating at an astounding pace—and to rate it as one of the most costly public health problems in the nation.[67] Like illegal drugs available from the dope dealer on the street, abuse of prescription medications is progressive and, given time, grows in severity. I heard someone describe it as the "hidden epidemic."

Addiction is the physical or mental dependence on a substance or behavior that a person feels he can't stop. For clarification, mental dependence includes emotional dependence.

Dependence is reliance on a mind altering substance for the purpose of changing feelings, or improving perception of difficult circumstances, or for reinforcement to live with oneself and others. In abuse of prescription drugs, reliance may be for any of the reasons I've mentioned plus the purpose for which it was prescribed. For example, pain pills for management, reduction, and elimination of pain used to the extent that the person feels powerless to stop.

M. T. knew this—all of this.

He was not like the man whose life was decimated by cocaine and, as a result, lost family, home, Jaguar, a $250,000-a-year position, and a place to lay his head other than on (or under) a park bench or in a remote corner at the train station.

No, M. T. was different. He was aware that the body is a divine gift. He did not have any problem with the scriptures about it being the temple of the Holy Spirit. He wasn't a dummy when it came to the damage caused by destructive habits.

Still, M. T. was in bondage to pain pills.

It started when he suffered a serious back injury that required several surgeries. Later, the problem switched into high gear when some adversities were allowed to get the upper hand. M. T. actually continued to live reasonably well and managed to hide it from his family for awhile. Eventually, members recognized that M. T. was on what Corinne Roosevelt Robinson described as "a path that leads to Nowhere"[68] and demonstrated it. On one occasion, his wife gathered up all the pills she could find and flushed them down the commode!

Five Guidebook Answers—Toward an Opening at the End of the Tunnel

1. Forget pedigree, social status, money.

Abuse can be classified under two headings. One is process addiction: gambling, spending, sexual activity, and eating. The other is substance addiction: alcohol, smoking, drugs, and prescriptions.

It's possible for a person to have multiple addictions. M. T. combined prescriptions with alcohol—potentially, a deadly combination. "I loved Margaritas," he confessed. "One and two became three and four which graduated into a pitcher. On occasions, a big pitcher . . . and more than one!"

Whether substance or process, addictions are an equal opportunity enemy. It makes no difference whether a person is prosperous or a pauper, under class, no class or upper class, a respectable member of the community drugging himself in the privacy of a million-dollar home on a manicured estate or a street person shooting it up in a dark alley across the railroad tracks. The substance may be hard core, or recreational, or available at the corner store, or one prescribed by a physician. (Sounds so respectable, doesn't it?)

No matter how it is dressed, the condition is similar. It is addiction, pure and simple. And it tells a story of misdirection, lost direction, no direction, lack of self-control, and a vacuum inside as big as the hole in the ozone layer.

2. Favor new surroundings.

Causes of PDA have been the center of much discussion and debate. Some claim that it is a brain disease that leads to persistent changes in brain structure and function.[69] Others counter with the claim that genetic predisposition may contribute to addictions.[70]

However, research insists that environmental influences are at the top of the list of powerful contributions to addiction. Recent research found that "social learning is the most influential single factor leading to addiction—family, subculture, advertising and media hype, and peer pressure."[71]

Since social learning feeds addiction, addicts should decide to change their surroundings. Some of their associations should end, and their circle of influence has to be adjusted. Since there is so much emotional and spiritual power in associations, it is critical to start filling that space in life with conditions and people who help solve the problem.

Don't quibble over it or second guess it. M. T. was advised, "Start, keep going, don't look back."

3. Forge a Freedom Partnership.

Whatever the causes of an addiction, the role of the addict is inescapable. It is not only improbable, it is probably impossible for the person who allowed himself to become addicted, to single-handedly free himself from the addiction.

These causes are very important, yet the addict needs something more than family, friends, and medical and mental science. Addiction is demonic, and the demon releases a destructive force on the victim's total health and higher reason for being on earth. It mounts a withering assault on faith and values.

Arrival at the opening at the end of the tunnel involves dependence, not on a substance, but on a Savior—the supernatural God. This isn't a crack pot, off-the-wall notion.

In my view, everyone depends on someone or some thing. Some depend on self-adequacy, knowledge, education, self-righteousness, the forces at work around the person, doubt, fear, science, status, the idea of "what will be, will be," and ignorance. I have known non-believers who depend on unbelief, agnostics who depend on an idea that it is impossible to prove God exists, and atheists who depend on no god.

Everyone depends on something or someone, yet not everyone depends on the One who has the most strength and supply for the need at hand. Each one could.

Think of receiving a note from the Almighty that reads: "You deserve better. I made you for the higher way. Your Friend, God."

Lines from the pen of Louisa Fletcher have been favorites of mine for a long time because they express the inner longing and need I am talking about.

I wish there were some wonderful place
Called the Land of Beginning Again,
Where all our mistakes and all our heartaches
And all of our poor selfish grief
Could be dropped like a shabby old coat at the door,
And never be put on again.[72]

A Freedom Partnership is not limited to a one-time-for-all-time spurt. It is a partnership for each day. Many have kept a Partnership Affirmation close by for use: God provides the strength I need. God is here to help me. I will depend on God. I will succeed.

4. Forgive Failure.

Jesus shared a basic truth of life when He said, "If you do not forgive others who fail you, the Heavenly Father will not forgive you" (Matt. 6:15). In the most famous sermon ever delivered, those words came after the model prayer: "Forgive us for the sins we have committed as we have forgiven the sins others have committed against us" (Matt. 6:12).

One way of looking at it is: We are forgiven to the extent we forgive others. Another way: We forgive others because we are forgiven. However, neither explains what I am now talking about, although they do lay the foundation.

With an addiction, as well as any failure, the addict also needs to forgive *himself*.

I am privileged to have known legions of people who have no problem with the idea of divine forgiveness. They have accepted it as regularly as the rising of the sun.

I have also witnessed the transformed relationship that occurs when people forgave others. And I have seen doubt and reluctance—in fact, stubborn resistance—at the idea of forgiving oneself.

It isn't uncommon to associate self-forgiveness with self-centeredness and self-aggrandizement. To the contrary, I find that divine forgiveness and self-forgiveness are like ice cream and cookies—they go together—and divine forgiveness makes the other possible and practical. After all, anyone who forgives himself is only doing what God has done—forgiven him.

There is also another dimension to it—divine forgiveness becomes fullest reality only when accompanied by self-forgiveness. Emotional, social, physical, and daily life—spiritual aliveness, too—depend on it. One of two dynamic spiritual principles is at work:

- Forgive failure—and failure will forgive you, or
- Fail to forgive—and the future, as well as failure, will not forgive you.

Therefore:

If a start was made toward the end of the tunnel, then stopped—forgive.

If noble intentions turned sour—forgive.

If promises have been broken—forgive.

If the wagon left the barn with you on it, but you fell off along the way—forgive.

ONCE FALLEN, THE MOST CRIPPLING DAMAGE IS NOT CAUSED BY THE FALL— IT IS CAUSED BY FAILURE TO SEEK AND ACCEPT FORGIVENESS, TO FORGIVE ONESELF, AND TO RISE AFTER FAILURE!

5. Fan the future.

Over the years, I have urged people to ask: "For what will I live the rest of my life—starting when?"

The answer is much more important than what a person has lived for up to that moment and what has been done prior to now. A satisfactory answer—one that moves the person toward the opening at the end of the tunnel—starts today for a satisfactory tomorrow. An unsatisfactory answer drags an unsatisfactory today into what will undoubtedly be an unsatisfactory tomorrow.

M. T. found his "Land of Beginning Again." The journey continues, not without challenges, but never without resources.

He asked the Lord to help.

> God did.
> He still asks.
> God still helps.
> M. T. isn't pain-free, but he is free from addiction—
> prescriptions and alcohol.
> The *alleluia* you hear?
> That's coming from M. T.
> And the other jubilant sound?
> That's coming from me.

A. P. S.
(Author's Postscript)

The use of prescription drugs for non-medical reasons is concentrated in three categories. One is pain relievers—OxyContin and Vicodin are popular pain relief drugs of choice among abusers. They also affect parts of the brain where pleasure is sensed.

Another category is sedatives and tranquilizers that address anxiety, tension, stress, and panic attacks. Xanax and Valium are in this family. Stimulants make up the third group—Ritalin and Dexedrine are well-known members that increase alertness, attention capabilities, and energy.

Like cocaine, marijuana, and tobacco, use of prescription drugs over long periods of time lead to loss of willpower (a person falls to the wrath of the drug), increased tolerance for the medication (takes stronger doses to achieve desired results), more frequent use (becomes a habit), and out of control behavior.

Millions are affected by prescription drug use, but recent trends raise big red flags, especially among older adults, adolescents, and women.

Emotional dependence usually embraces physical addiction to constitute a double whammy—a body and mind duo. However, I have seen a separation of the two. For instance, people who have stopped smoking, yet long after the craving for nicotine left, there were times when they really wanted to light up.

My father smoked unfiltered cigarettes starting at a very young age. In his forties, he kicked the addiction completely. In his seventies, he admitted, "I could light up another one in a heartbeat and enjoy it." An emotional connection was still present.

Whether physical, or mental-emotional, or both, addiction is treatable and defeatable.

Discussion Room

Agree	Disagree	
☐	☐	The only thing M. T. needed to do to overcome addiction was to depend on the Lord.
☐	☐	Physicians, health care providers, and pharmacists could be sure that patients or clients don't have access to more drugs than they should.
☐	☐	A stable family is the most effective tool to prevent abuse.*
☐	☐	Process addiction (gambling, spending, eating) isn't as bad as substance addiction (alcoholism, drug, prescriptions, smoking).
☐	☐	Too much stir is made about the feelings of pleasure produced by drugs.
☐	☐	Changed behavior changes the person.**
☐	☐	The church ought to welcome people who have addiction problems.
☐	☐	It would be better to grin and bear pain than to take medication which could become addictive.
☐	☐	Addicted people are weaklings and possess criminal tendencies.***
☐	☐	Anybody who trusts God doesn't need any other help to make his life right.
☐	☐	Older people who abuse drugs have earned whatever pleasures they derive from the addiction.

Agree	Disagree	
☐	☐	Everyone needs a Xanax once in awhile to deal with stresses in life.
☐	☐	If prescription medicines weren't good for us, God would not allow them to be developed.
☐	☐	Each person is the captain of his fate, the master of his soul.
☐	☐	Faith and things spiritual apply to mind and body, as well as soul.

*Yes [73] **Not by itself [74] ***Not necessarily[75]

So They Say—Prescription Drug Abusers on Main Street America

- What began as a necessity (control pain during recuperation from surgery) continued as a necessity (due to misuse and overuse) after there wasn't any medical reason for it.
- After taking one pill—just *one*—I was hooked on the pleasure I felt.
- I can see where I could have become addicted, if I had not followed directions and stopped when I should.
- Something I can see (a pill) is needed to help me deal with something I can feel, but can't see (low opinion of self). Anything wrong with that?
- Don't be too hard on it (a specific medication) . . . I love it . . . Wouldn't do without it!
- You ask if getting the drug is a challenge? You've got to be kidding! It's as easy as getting a loaf of bread at the store a few blocks away.
- I became an expert on how to quit smoking—did it seventeen times.
- I get drugs from eight medical providers (each one unaware of the others).
- Take it from me. A (prescription) drug addict can kick it. No one could have a more serious problem than I did.

- My son brought me to my knees when he said, "Mom, I love pot. You love Valium. What makes you feel you're better than me?"
- A combination of faith, church, friends, and the Lord made the difference for me.

Prayer to Move Toward the Opening at the End of the Tunnel

Transforming Savior, manifest Your presence to those who are captive to addictions and cleanse self-depreciation with redemptive thoughts. When dedication is feeble, remind them that there is still time to get on the way toward fullness.

Provide help, mighty God, to believe that there is no condition beyond assistance, and that they can rediscover completeness, even if health and finances have been lost.

Assure them that the causes for their anxieties can be resolved. Arouse in them the willingness to trust You for the power equal to that which brought Jesus from the grave long ago.

Supply insight, determination, frankness, and gentleness to all who work for their recovery.

Also bless family members and friends with a patience that won't give up and a love that refuses to quit. Feelings are terribly exasperating at times, Lord. You are aware of the frustrations. Especially during those moments, dispense tenacious grace for them to be supportive without being enablers and courage to make those who are addicted accountable for their actions. Through Him whose mercy makes the difference. Amen.

Good News

They brought to Jesus many who were enslaved by demons and He cast those spirits out (Matt. 8:16).

---

Chapter Thirteen

*Did a Twenty-one day Forward into
the Past Plan Make Any Difference?*

Peggy and Jeff, Next Stop—Divorce Court!

Mark Twain said that the announcement of his demise was premature. So are predictions about the death of marriage. According to information from the U.S. Census Bureau, 95 percent of us have been married by the time we reach mid-life.[76] Furthermore, the divorce rate has declined in recent years.

No doubt, one reason is a decline in the percentage of the population that is married—over the last thirty-five years, it has dropped from 72 percent to 52 percent. It is also reasonable to conclude that the dramatic spike in couples opting for cohabitation is another factor. They live like married couples, but aren't. As a result, the divorce rate doesn't take a hit when there is a break-up.

But one fact is indisputable: Problems among marriage partners haven't lost their clout. I have observed that the ones most likely to threaten a marriage often stem from:

- Loss of purpose for marriage to the present spouse—"The reasons I married him/her no longer exist."
- Decreased significance of marriage to the present spouse—"I'm not getting as much out of it as I need" . . . "I'm putting a lot more into it than I'm receiving from it."

- Diminished value of marriage to the husband or wife—"I can do without him/her" . . . "I can do better than what I've got."

Unresolved, issues like these lead to one of two outcomes: The marriage is considered a creeping failure, but a decision is made, for one reason or another, to continue the façade—"I'll put up with it" (whatever the "it" may be). Consignment to failure, in turn, could lead to a proxy marriage, an extramarital affair, maybe many affairs, in which someone other than the marriage partner becomes a stand-in for the spouse.

The other possible outcome is to throw in the towel: "I don't think this marriage is worth any further investment of my time, resources, and self." "There's much more to life . . . surely there is . . . there must be . . . and I've got to get out there."

Nineteen years and a couple of children later, neither Peggy nor Jeff was in a proxy marriage, but their relationship was in marital ICU. If anyone had asked them whether they felt that God has a hand in bringing people together, in less time than it takes to blink an eye they would have answered, "Yes."

Anybody who invited them to explain their dilemma would have heard replies like: "We're too different now." "We've grown apart." "We no longer feel a need for each other" (both were in successful careers).

And what about their problems? "Peggy, Jeff, do you feel they were avoidable?" Without hesitating as long as it takes to blush, each would have answered in the affirmative. "Is the marriage salvageable?" "Why should it be saved?" "Well, ____?"

Eight Guidebook Answers— Going for the Gold

1. Re-evaluate marriage.

In most societies, it officially begins with a wedding, but a wedding does not a marriage make. *Relationship does!* Even amid all the hoopla, excitement, pomp, and circumstance (also expense for some—not long ago, a couple spent $15 million on the daughter's wedding!), the wedding is merely a visible ritual by which two people mark a beginning of life together.

When all that hoopla, excitement, pomp, and circumstance simmer down, what is left standing? Two people and life together at the starting gate. I know many successful couples that were together for a long while, before this reality sank in.

MARRIAGE = RELATIONSHIP DEVELOPED BY PROGRESSIVE UNION . . . TOGETHER.

From a practical point of view, marriage can be described as *relationship* developed by a *progressive union* in which two people unite lives through working, dreaming, thinking, talking, doing, problem-solving, laughing, crying, forgiving, achieving, and loving *together*.

A relationship helps a couple to keep their eye on the ball—marriage as it is *intended* to be. With the wedding as the start of the race, marriage becomes the process of running it. Seldom have I witnessed threatening problems at the starting gate, but problems have many, disruptive, and cunning ways to crop up during the run.

2. Reconsider compatibility—with *Marriage*.

Incompatibility is at the top of the list as a cause of divorce. "We just aren't right for each other." "We're like mixing oil and water." "We don't like each other anymore." These refer to an inability to get along with one another. Personal compatibility is important, but at the moment I am not talking about one another.

Rather I am speaking of compatibility with *marriage* itself. Is the married person and marriage getting along? Some questions could provide the answer.

- Do I now agree with marriage?
- Does marriage agree with me?
- Do I like marriage—really?
- Could I learn to like it—again?
- What will it take for marriage and me to become friends?

163

Anyone unable or unwilling to deal satisfactorily with what has been discussed thus far probably will not see much sense in the remaining 6 Guidebook Answers.

3. Reassess value—not of marriage, but of your *husband/ wife*.

Put the value of marriage on hold for a moment. Since value of persons should always trump all other considerations, the value of marriage can be determined best when the value of one to the other is cleared up.

How valuable is the spouse—to *you*? What are his/her strengths as a person, not weaknesses, but strengths? (Save weaknesses for another day.)

In your eyes, what strengths do you feel you have? The value placed on the spouse has impact—enormous impact—on him/her. But at the same time, it says something loud and clear about the value placed on yourself. It is true that a person tends to see others in the way he sees himself and to think of others in the way he thinks of himself.

The Scriptures puts it this way: The one who loves his or her spouse, loves himself (Eph. 5:28). One who values husband or wife as a person values himself.

At some point in the past, you made a commitment to your spouse that indicated you valued that person. Maybe you didn't realize that the integrity of yourself was at stake, and still is.

So, think about these points again—the value of your spouse and your value as persons.

4. Resurrect what could be.

Apply I-Would-Like-For-It-To-Be, a spiritual principle that combines what a person needs with what God is prepared to give. It is done by circling the need with what the person believes to be the answer. Here's an example.

One time, a prominent person in the community said to Jesus, "My child is nearly dead." That was his reality—a child on death's doorstep. When he continued, "Come and make her well," he circled the reality, a child near death, with "I-would-like-for-it-to-be." What to him was the answer? Wellness for his child (Mark 5:22–24). It is not presumptuous, assumptuous, or a version of any name and claim notion.

Applied to marriage, here's what I mean.

Marriage could be healthy again—"I-would-like-for-it-to-be."

The relationship could be a source of joy again—"I-would-like-for-it-to-be."

Changes that help return harmony to the relationship can be made—"I-would-like-for-it-to-be."

Adjustments that would go a long way to restoring the marriage to prosperity could become reality—"I-would-like-for-it-to-be."

The spirit of I-would-like-for-it-to-be will go the second and third mile to solve problems in marriage. *Put it to work and it will work for everyone involved.*

5. Repair downed communications lines.

The Amish people in Pennsylvania, Ohio, Indiana, and other areas of America are children of the separatist movement in Europe several hundred years ago. They are called the "Plain People." I have found them to be fascinating and very special folk, the kind you could bet your life on.

Many of the Amish shun modern luxuries that most of us think we can't live without. Have you seen them riding in their black horse-drawn buggies? I did, not long ago—teenagers on a picturesque country road. The horse was in a full gallop and the covering over the buggy was folded down. When I saw them later, they said that it was their special convertible buggy!

Modern conveniences aren't all that is shunned. They also shun their folk who seriously stray from the accepted way. It is a form of community discipline that is exceptionally effective.

When the decision has been made to shun someone until he or she returns to the way, there is no further association with the person. Communication in any form is forbidden. I have been told that of the many methods used in shunning, lack of communication has the most severe impact. "It is devastating," a leader said.

Lack of communication is also devastating to a marriage. It is one of the primary reasons couples drift apart and break up. After the divorce, someone looked back and said, "We finally stopped talking—not suddenly, but gradually. It just happened."

COMMUNICATION IS MORE THAN MAKING A SOUND

Communication includes talking, but there is more to communication than sound coming from the mouth. A person can speak endlessly and never say anything.

Communication includes conversation that *makes a difference.*

Small talk has its contribution to make, but healthy relationship requires more. Talk with substance to it—that is a mark of healthy marriages. How does a person begin to repair downed lines of communications?

Combine initiation (first step) and congratulations (a show of support) with communications (sharing verbally)—they make-up a holy trinity in successful marriages. Go ahead and take the first step by throwing in a sincere compliment or two. Works like these pave the way for words to be believable.

Sideline disagreements for the moment—but don't sweep them under the rug; reserve them for a more appropriate time. Remember, there is a time and place for all things honest and good. In the beginning, share matters on which agreement is possible. The beginning point for one couple was trivial stuff, and it worked. From there they were able to progress to meatier issues.

6. Rebuild friendship with realism.

Some elements manifested during the early years of marriage ended after a while. At least, they should have. Success in marriage does *not* depend on the euphoric bliss that comes in spurts, or the fireworks that light up the matrimonial sky occasionally, or the moments of ecstasy enjoyed sporadically.

As routine (and dull) as it may seem, success is determined not by the spectacular times in life, but by handling favorably the day in and day out realities that are inevitable in life together. After fourteen years of marriage, a thirty-something couple said, "Only when we revisited this matter of realism for us, and accepted it, did our relationship take on a sustainable growth." Something else happened. "Our reality brought fresh meaning to the moments of 'bliss, fireworks (and) ecstasy'!"

ALERT: DON'T LET HARSH REALITIES LEAD INTO MAKING HASTY JUDGMENTS AND RASH DECISIONS ABOUT MARRIAGE.

7. Reenergize relationship with *Just for You Moments.*

A *Just For You Moment* is an occasion reserved exclusively for the husband or wife, no one else. For a stay-at-home mom, one of those moments consists of fifteen minutes reserved for her husband when he arrives home. During this time, she finds out how his day went. The children know that they are to leave their parents alone unless they are suffering one of the four B's—bleeding, barfing, broken bone, not breathing.

What are some reasons *Just For You Moments* help build relationship? The emphasis is one-on-one, not one-on-a-crowd or a crowd-on-a-crowd. The exclusive nature encourages a feeling that "I'm special to him/her," a feeling everyone needs. *Just For You Moments* also reinforce self-esteem, a characteristic every couple needs, but many have lost.

Do something thoughtful for your spouse—*this* week. It doesn't have to be elaborate or break the bank, but it should show sincerity and thoughtfulness. Furthermore, it isn't necessary to wait until a birthday or anniversary. In fact, a *Just For You Moment* when there is no special occasion makes it more special.

The husband in one of my favorite couples has found a remarkable, yet, simple way that works. He calls it Mystery Surprises—"surprise her with a surprise," he explained. Occasionally, the surprise is an outing, half-day, full day, or overnight—something he knows she will enjoy, but he does not tell her the destination or features. By nature, she has more curiosity than what it takes to kill the cat. She always wants to know where they are going and what they will do when they get there. He may reply with answers like, "Well, we're not going to Tokyo." "We'll probably not see the Pope on this trip." Answers are truthful and obviously unrealistic.

You can only imagine the interest these surprises have generated and their value to the relationship. What may seem more remarkable is that they began after the couple had been married for many years!

ADVISORY: MAKE A SERIOUS ATTEMPT NOT TO ACT SO SHOCKED THE FIRST FEW TIMES YOU ARE TREATED TO *JUST FOR YOU MOMENTS.* THEY SHOULD THRILL, NOT KILL, A PERSON!

8. Rekindle relationship—Twenty-one Day Forward into the Past Plan.

Day 1–7: Once each day, think about times in the past when the relationship was at the top of its game—at least, better than it is now. Jot down when they occurred, what you were doing, and other thoughts that come to mind. Include the causes for the healthy relationship and what they brought to the table to make it that way.

The first seven days focus on the positives, not the negatives, at work in the marriage at the moment.

Day 8–14: Share findings, one each day, with the spouse. Invite input by asking, "What do you think?" "How does this strike you?" And *listen* to one another. It might not hurt to also ask, "Want to do something like it again?"

Day 15–21: As much as possible, do a "something like it" each day, or two, or three, or four—well, at least once during the seven days!

- Be sensible.
- Respect the ordinary.
- Offer and accept forgiveness.
- Attempt the extraordinary.
- Expect noticeable results.

Far from living in the past, these actions fast forward the past into the present for the purpose of making the present better than it is now. Don't be surprised when there is re-found meaning, acceptance, and happiness. When needed, repeat the Plan.

Are you worth it? Is your husband or wife? What about others in the family—children, parents, or grandchildren?

If God has anything to say about it, I'm positive I hear Him saying, "You bet they're worth it!"

"All of them!"

The next stop for Peggy and Jeff appeared to be divorce court. They were already at the door. Before walking through it, they wisely agreed to give serious thought to their lives, future, family, faith, and the investment they had already made in one another. Only then did they find themselves ready to make a fresh commitment to each other.

They told me that the Twenty-one Day Forward into the Past Plan and I-Would-Like-for-It-to-Be Principle made the most difference for them.

In time, they became stronger persons and believers. An interesting thing happened along the way—their relationship spread new wings.

I have reason to think that some sparks and barks returned to it.

And that God is proud of them.

I know I am.

A. P. S.
(Author's Postscript)

One of the most popular reasons people say they marry is love—"I love him/her." But what do you suppose is meant by the word "love"?

Care—"I care for (the person)." Attraction—"I'm attracted to him/her." Feeling—"I have feelings for _____." But are any of these synonyms for love? No. The closest one to it would be "care." Although love is one of the hardest things in the world to define, it must be more than any of these words.

Notice the emphasis on feelings. Now, let's go a couple of steps further.

If a person doesn't feel that he cares any longer for the spouse, is it necessary to stop kindness, thoughtfulness, and special moments?

Do deeds and words of love need to stop when feelings of love stop? For instance, can a person no longer say "I love you" when he doesn't feel that he loves at the moment it is said?

People in various areas of the world have differing customs. Take Finland. A Finn told me that seldom do couples say they love each other. "Oh, it may be whispered on the death bed, but don't count on it." He smiled.

In America, it's a different story.

It's possible that too much ado is made about feeling love. And it isn't uncommon for love to be determined by the presence or absence of warm, gushy feelings. Then it should be no surprise when a feeling may be mistaken for being in love and an absence of feeling as "we no longer love each other." There's more.

In marriage, must a person feel love to behave in a loving way? The inclination embedded in our psyche is to say, "Yes." Then, is a person a hypocrite if he acts and speaks in ways that are consistent with love when he does not feel the way he talks and walks? Our culture is apt to answer that he is.

Principle of Opposite Behavior

As I see it, both are a mistake and contradict the Principle of Opposite Behavior that Jesus taught. "You have heard that it is OK to hate your enemies, but I say, love even your enemies" (Matt. 5:43–44). Here, love is more than a feeling. It is an act and word that agrees with the principle of love. "Do good to those who hate you."

There are times in life, certainly in marriage, when behavior not supported by feeling is needed, right, and justified. Then it is true that love can be spoken and shown when it is not accompanied by a warm, chummy, all-is-right-with-the-world feeling—without being two-faced.

Discussion Room

Agree	Disagree	
☐	☐	Marriage will turn an unhappy person into a happy person.
☐	☐	Couples need interests different from one another.
☐	☐	Separate lives—vacations, outings, bank accounts, hobbies—are okay.
☐	☐	Lots of money would cure most problems couples have.
☐	☐	Having a child will solve problems in a marriage.
☐	☐	On its best day, marriage is work.
☐	☐	Problem marriages seldom fix themselves.
☐	☐	Spiritual faith has a lot to do with resolving conflicts in marriages.
☐	☐	Face it—some people shouldn't have married.
☐	☐	A spouse should understand when the boss demands more of the partner's time.
☐	☐	With life the way it is these days, problems in marriages are inevitable.
☐	☐	Couples wouldn't have as many problems if they didn't have kids.
☐	☐	The role of intimacy has been exaggerated.
☐	☐	Romance and real love are not the same.
☐	☐	The person I married is not the one I thought I was getting.
☐	☐	Personal appearance does not affect a marriage one way or the other.

Agree	Disagree	
☐	☐	It's better to steer clear of marital disagreements or arguments or fights.
☐	☐	If I had it to do over, I would marry the same person.

Fourteen You're-Headed-For-Danger Signs

- Silence—failure to communicate or lack of meaningful conversation
- Satisfaction with status quo—more comfortable with the way things are
- Declining time for or with one another—absence of quality time together
- Neglect—lack of personal or exclusive attention
- Forgetfulness—special occasions (birthdays, anniversaries, etc.,) pass unnoticed
- Fatal Attraction—welcoming romantic hints or attention or flirting from person(s) other than the marriage partner
- Weasel Response—too weak or unwilling to nip in the bud advances by someone who isn't the spouse
- I'm The Champ Syndrome—need to come out on top of disagreements or arguments
- Absence of physical intimacy—when there is no plausible explanation
- Narrow concept of intimacy—discounts role of cuddling, touching, kissing, embracing
- Avoidance—sidestep issues or problems
- Wave the White Flag Maneuver—no longer strives to improve the relationship
- Faith Stagnation—declining or loss of spiritual alertness in daily life

Prayer for Couples

Lord, gracious Shepherd, come to couples experiencing problems with a new willingness to forgive each other. Speak the value of relationship to them again. Soften hard hearts. Break the chain around an unyielding attitude, and weaken the grip of uncompromising pride.

Open hearts and minds to healing for the divisions that separate them while generously endowing them with renewed confidence, understanding, and the inclination to work at honest marriage enrichment.

Engrave on their hearts, Eternal One, Your claim of grace so powerfully that all other claims may be subjugated in love. Pull them to life-changing mercies and re-ignite the embers of romance. Thank You for being where they are to bring these blessings. In the name of the great Reconciler. Amen.

Good News

Let nothing be done from a self-centered ambition or through deception; humbly consider one another in the way you would like to be considered. Both of you should look out for the other's interests, as well as your own. Work on your frame of mind to align it with the attitude Jesus showed (Phil. 2:3–5).

Chapter Fourteen

Sinking thinking ability followed by complete collapse—it's enough to make grown people cry.

Dementia Stole Lucille's Mind—Her Life, Too!

There are many faces to dementia including Huntington's Disease. But the most well-known form is probably Alzheimer's. According to the National Institute of Health, over twenty-three million people in the United States alone suffer from the disease or have family members who do.[77] The number worldwide would probably jar the senses.

If forgetfulness and the tendency to be scatter-brained occasionally is any barometer, everyone is touched by a tad of dementia. Starting with infancy, there is a process of growth and dying at work in the body and mind. With age, functions of the mind tend to expand and contract.

At the same time, lack of memory in the forty-plus years could be no more severe than in younger years, but when they are younger, people are too busy putting bread on the table, rearing children, and taking in activities they enjoy the most, to remember that they are forgetful.

Still, changes in mental functions speed up with age and fruits of dementia may become more obvious. Many agree that Alzheimer's is its most extreme wing because it inflicts such a loss of mental and intellectual abilities that physical deterioration and death are hastened.

Lucille was one of the millions who suffered the dreaded disease.

She had been a salt-of-the-earth kind of person and a devoted believer who was very active in her church. Mention the women's work and her face would light up like a child in the toy store on Christmas Eve.

At first, little memory failures were no more uncommon than with other people. She took them in stride. So did her family. There didn't appear to be cause for alarm. But as time passed, forgetfulness, misplaced and displaced items used every day, unconcern about personal appearance, and loss of interest in personal hygiene became more frequent, serious, and noticeable.

The decline was not an overnight phenomenon, nor did it move at the speed of a slow boat to China. In time, however, the disease unleashed a furious assault on her.

Lucille's life was confined to a jumbled conglomeration of nothing days and yesteryears.

What could *family members* and a network of friends do?

And, "What Can I Do To Stay As Alert As I Can For As Long As I Can?"

Six Guidebook Answers— During Dementia's Night

1. Act real.

The loved one's condition is probably heartbreaking. In Lucille's case, her love, tenderness, understanding shown to her family, the times she put band-aids on scratches, gave aspirins to bring the fever down and, yes, dished out some discipline to her children could not be forgotten.

It's natural to recall how interested she was in problems and the ways she helped to make it over mountains that, at the moment, seemed like a Mt. Everest. Now, however, there is a new reality in town—and it is nearly unbearable. The loved one cannot repeat the name of family members, not even if life were to depend on it. The loved one stares directly at one who is near and dear, but there is no earthly idea who or what the person is.

"I'm just some unknown person who brings nice things," a daughter said about visits with her mother.

It's time to maintain composure anyway.

Hold the hand for a moment. Gently kiss on the cheek. Hug without squeezing.

Do a love-something for the person.

In this way, the real world of a family member meets the world that is real to the one who suffers dementia.

2. Act normal.

"How could anyone expect me to be normal in the presence of the one I love who is anything but normal?" a woman retorted.

It may not be easy. In fact, it may take extra effort. After all, the loved one's condition is abnormal, however, un-normal behavior around the person could accentuate the abnormal world in which he/she lives. A degree of behavior that is normal might help, but be careful not to confuse acting normal with denial.

While fully aware of the distressing condition, encourage an environment of life. It may have more impact on the person than first thought. Lucille's behavior after one of her children died indicates what I mean.

A "God-Sense"

The family did not feel there was any point in telling her. "She wouldn't understand," they reasoned, and, considering previous experience, they were right.

Yet, for a number of days following the child's death, Lucille's demeanor changed. She seemed troubled, uneasy, agitated, and sorrowful. After a week or two, it returned to what it had been prior to his death.

A perceptive observer insisted, "She knew! She knew! Somewhere inside her, she knew!"

Maybe she did—a "God sense," as a physician suggested, could have kicked-in.

Keep in mind that the normalcy which could make the atmosphere more tolerable for family members, and be a positive influence on the one who has dementia, depends on *family members,* not the condition of the one who is diseased. So, responsibility for trying rests with members of the family.

3. Act sensibly.

It is a hand-in-glove companion of normal behavior and takes into account the destructive effects dementia has on the conduct of the person. Conditions have changed. The loved one is not the way she/he was and, this side of heaven, will never again act as before. Therefore, exercise common sense by tailoring your responses to what the person says and does.

4. Act creatively.

Find ways to involve the loved one in conversation and activity. It may be necessary to go back to the person's childhood. Still, situations to stimulate a response can probably be created.

It is okay to engage in some make believe. Remember, a family member works with what is most real to the Lucille in the family.

For instance, when a father talked about times when he was a youngster, his son jumped in to take full advantage of the opportunity. He would make conversation of a sort out of them. They were brief. Only a minute or two was the limit of dad's capabilities. Experiences brought up by the father may have never happened. He could have been imagining them, but they were real to him at that moment. The son entered his father's world of the moment with make believe of his own by asking questions like, "How did you feel about _____?" "Were you glad that _____?" "Tell me what happened to _____."

If his father didn't respond, the creative son filled in an answer. He told me, "From what I could see, it meant something to dad—some of it did. There's no doubt that it did me some good."

5. Act dependently.

Dementia takes bigger and bigger bites out of a loved one's life. As it does, feelings of helplessness often descend on family members like heavy fog on the Great Smoky Mountains in early hours of the morning.

"I feel so helpless," a family attendant confessed.

In many demands of life, the need of one person becomes opportunity to give for another person. The demands Alzheimer's and other severe diseases like it present need (dependence on another) and opportunity (for another to help).

Seek help when you are at your wits end. Don't know what to do next? Ask someone who might know. You may need care from an out-of-the-family facility. Don't struggle with the issue; the well-being of the loved one is of paramount importance. It is okay to use a care center. The truth is, turning to professional care may be the smartest choice and best for the afflicted family member. But never—once more, *never*—forget the person. That is as close to the unpardonable sin in the family setting as anyone can come. However, before making a final decision, be sure to take the time and make the effort to check out centers carefully. Not all facilities are equal.

6. Act compassionately.

There are some things alert members of the family are able to do.

There are some things they are not able to do. But do not lose confidence! A person can do at the moment whatever needs to be done *at that moment*.

I have seen this guideline work dramatically: To the extent that I do what I can for the least able, I do as for the most able—God. And this personal love-guideline when family members are no longer able to do what they once did or what they once did is no longer helpful: As much as possible, I will find others who can provide the assistance needed. Now, I trust my loved one to the goodness and greatness of God.

"I DON'T WANT WHAT HAPPENED TO LUCILLE TO HAPPEN TO ME!"

Assume for a moment that you are blessed with thinking ability— your mind still functions, at least reasonably well. In jest, a friend expressed his doubts when he said, "Of all the things I've lost, I miss my mind the most."

I am sure that if I were to poll everyone reading this chapter, not a single one would want to give up mental alertness. No one in his right mind would—no pun intended—but as someone wondered out loud, "What can I do to prevent it, or at least to reduce the chances?"

Genetic make-up may dispose a person to dementia in which case Uncle Joe and Grandma Sally could have some influence. Other factors, and very powerful ones, include medical, social, practical, and spiritual stimulants that have impeded the advance of the sort of dementia that seriously disrupts life. A person can also help in ways that strengthen and lengthen awareness.

Ten Steps to Remain as Alert as You Can for as Long as You Can

1. Push Ground Zero Fears into a back room.

The likelihood of a person contracting debilitating dementia is so remote that Las Vegas odds-makers would not give a person the odds they would for him to win American Idol. Yet, there are people who are so obsessed with the fear of dementia that some meaningful living and adventures are scuttled.

I remember a family friend who refused to enjoy some perks which she could easily afford. "I will probably need the money to pay for nursing home care," she argued, "or some other unforeseen calamity." Of course, it is a possibility for anyone, but possibility doesn't make it an inevitable disease in the future.

A gerontologist in attendance at one of my meetings mentioned that a strong Ground Zero Fear could actually help bring on that which is feared. To me, the smartest way to approach the possibility of dementia—or any bad thing, for that matter—has a spiritual head on it. In short:

WITH GOD'S HELP, WHATEVER HAPPENS CAN BE HANDLED. IN THE MEANWHILE, I WILL L-I-V-E!

This approach is applicable to everyday, every tomorrow.

2. Accept garden variety dementia as natural as love for apple pie.

Have you ever met anyone totally free of some characteristics associated with dementia including, but not limited to:

"Oh, I forgot." (This reminds me of the woman who was asked if her husband remembered her birthday. "No," she answered, "he always forgets. I remind him in January and July.")

"Now, where did I put the keys?"

"Have you seen my books? glasses? lunch bag? pencils? socks? shoes?"

"Do you know where I put my purse?"

"Did you move my umbrella?"

"What did you say?"

"I was sure I did that."

"What happened to my cell phone?" "I don't know, dear." "You moved it." "No, I didn't." "You must have. It was right there." "For the last time, I haven't moved, taken, borrowed, or touched your cell phone." "Well, I'm sure you . . . oh, here it is."

You haven't come across anyone who is characteristic-free, have you? Neither have I. To be bothered by the everyday stuff is a waste of good mental and emotional energy. It is also a waste of time.

3. Intermingle face-to-face with others.

A sociologist friend and I were talking about isolation in society as a creeping problem and the heavy price it imposes on its victims. One idea that was shared is the unnecessary uses of new technologies.

People are able to communicate without ever seeing one another eyeball-to-eyeball. There is not even a trace of in-person, warm-blooded contact. E-mail has many positive uses, but how many times is it used when a person could just as easily pick-up the telephone and talk to a real, breathing human being? And what about text messaging when nothing would suffer by making a direct appearance?

Then there is Mighty T—television. Fanatical use of it glorifies a great modern goddess—Remote Participation. All comfy in a favorite chair, click the button, say nothing, do nothing, think nothing, feel nothing, and become nothing while watching nothing much of the time.

Oh, well, nothing gained, nothing lost!

Wait a moment. Maybe something is lost, something of incredible value—physical, social, emotional, and spiritual wholeness—being offered as a sacrificial lamb on the altar of twenty-first century goddess, Remote Participation. Social scientists who believe that isolation becomes a plague when it is on the loose in a person's life have my undivided attention.

Remote Participation can be considered a deadly virus that inflicts damages on the whole person far greater than the decimation of the poultry population when a hungry wolf runs wild in the hen house.

As a person gets older, the effects of isolation become more severe, and one of them is on thinking capacity.

GET INTO LIFE—AND LIFE WILL FIND A WAY TO GET TO YOU!

Whatever your age, there is a lot of life out there. Believe it. Get out there and life has a way of getting to you. Get out there and you could lessen the growth of dementia's characteristics and slow down its expansion.

- Worship—with other people.
- Church—with other people.
- Social gatherings—with other people.
- Family activities—with other people.
- Community involvement—with other people.
- Neighborhood events—with other people.

181

- Concerts, sporting events, card games, a day at the park, the museum, the planetarium, the zoo, dinners—with other people.

But there is a reverse reality.

STAY AWAY FROM LIFE—AND LIFE WILL FIND A WAY TO STAY AWAY FROM YOU!

4. Stimulate thought processes.

Every day engage in an activity other than what you do for a living—an activity that requires you to think. It could be a game, puzzle, a book, helpful saying, or a walk. I know a man who exercises by walking. During his walks, he puts a word to each step; for instance, 2—zoo, 10—friend, 2-0-mow, 5-0-go. He told me that in time, hundreds of words have come to mind. "It's fun; it stretches my mind, and I'm doing a good thing, all at the same time."

In "Last Word" at the end of this book, I mention that I have made it my business to read what others write and listen to what they say. At times, I have not agreed with them, but I discovered that if they caused me to think, the effort was worth it.

The Use Principle is true and works:

YOU COULD LOSE WHAT YOU DO NOT USE.

5. Take advantage of advances in medicine.

Researchers are doing a remarkable job coming up with new discoveries that can improve thinking processes and delay a more serious collapse into dysfunctional dementia, maybe for as long as you live. Some hold out promise of at least a partial repair of capabilities. Talk to your physician. Go on-line and to the local library where an abundance of information is available.

6. Take lapses in stride.

Why fret when a word is not on the tip of the tongue? Don't worry about it. Have some fun—chalk it up to a "Senior Moment," or

"Mid-Life Moment," or "Thirty-Something Moment," or "Whatever-Your-Age Moment" and go on to something else. Besides, it may come to mind later. If not, fall back on a wise grandmother's advice: Forget? Don't regret. "Probably it wasn't worth remembering anyway."

7. Accept help with head up, shoulders straight.

Dementia comes with its own slate of unique challenges, and none is more obvious than the need for help from a wide range of sources. Professionals, spiritual advisors, family, and caring friends are among them. Instead of withdrawing, open your hands and stretch them out to receive. Be thankful that someone is willing, ready, and trained to be of assistance; it shows that you are special.

8. Pay attention to life's pluses.

Of course, there are negatives, but life is better lived on the pluses. There is more enjoyment in the life that thinks and moves on the upside. There is more strength given to those who refuse to allow negatives to overpower them.

9. Trust the day after today to God.

Above all others, the Lord will be where you are going when you get there with everything you could possibly need when you arrive. Others have found it is true, and you can depend on God to do the same for you.

10. Renew the Covenant Connection.

In the chapter, Elaine, Child Of Believers (And God)—Lost In A Wilderness, I discuss the Covenant Connection between God and His people. In this chapter, I want to make the application age-, mind-, and body-specific.

What is the divine Covenant with a person? God pledges His *full* resources to be *your* God all the time, everywhere, and in *any condition* life throws at you—for as long as **GOD** lives.

Age is no barrier or disadvantage to God. Neither is condition of mind and body. I know a lot of people, like Shirley and Al, who say, "God keeps a blind eye to things like those!"

Matt agrees, "They got that right."

A. P. S.
(Author's Postscript)

Until the cure for dementia is developed, I suppose the main objective is control. But there is another side of it pointed out by a new study that caught my attention.

For some time, research has argued that being overweight in mid-life increases the chances of developing dementia in later years. The most recent study adds that there is a higher than average risk from "storing a lot of fat in the abdomen."[78] The presence of a "lot of fat in the abdomen" doesn't arbitrarily make anyone overweight. However, scientific findings indicate that its presence in forty-something people, for example, make them more susceptible to dementia when they're in their seventies.

Researchers have pointed out for some time the link between fat and risk of diabetes, stroke, and heart disease. Dr. Rachel Whitmer of the Kaiser Permanent Division of Research made it clear that with abdominal fat, "We can add dementia."

Piled on top of contributing factors like use of tobacco products, undisciplined menu or eating habits, lack of exercise, and uncontrolled blood pressure, there's the "beer belly" factor—or some semblance to it. A disorderly life cracks open the door to a flood of ailments. Somewhere in the Scriptures, isn't there a word about the body being the temple of the Holy Spirit?

Discussion Room

Agree	Disagree	
☐	☐	There are stages in life. Old age is one of them.
☐	☐	Dementia is an old folk's disease.
☐	☐	A compassionate society requires that all citizens join hands to provide for those who are unable to provide for themselves.

Agree	Disagree	
☐	☐	With life the way it is nowadays, family members don't have time to be responsible for aged parents or grandparents.
☐	☐	The role of government includes health care for its citizens.
☐	☐	It may rain on the just and the unjust, but the unjust get wetter.
☐	☐	Financial demands of daily life make it impossible to care for loved ones suffering Alzheimer's.
☐	☐	If the church did its job, there wouldn't be any need for public or governmental assistance programs.
☐	☐	When you get down to it, life is unfair.
☐	☐	The expense of health care is unnecessary. Let nature take its course.
☐	☐	I wish my church were more involved in ministries to special-needs persons and families.
☐	☐	Most people could do more to prevent suffering from diseases like dementia.
☐	☐	There are things worse than death.
☐	☐	Believers need to get more involved in solving problems in the community.
☐	☐	It's possible for a person to give God thanks, no matter what happens.

Prayer for God's Children Whose Lives Are in a Fog of Forgetfulness

Dear God, hear the prayers they cannot pray. Listen to the songs they cannot sing. Comfort them with scriptures they cannot read. Reward the faith they cannot express.

Cheer them by visitors they do not recognize. Encourage them by children they have forgotten. Let them feel the love of the companion they can no longer call by name.

Give them your peace in the mysterious place where they have gone away from us. Do not forsake them in their desert of forgetfulness and total dependency. Abide with them until that glorious moment when you take them into your eternal presence where their memory will be restored.

And they can again sing your praises.

And they will walk again with dignity.

And they will talk again with clarity.

And they will know all things even as they are known. In Jesus name. Amen.

(Offered by Eula Williams at the dedication of a special care unit in South Carolina)

Good News

I am the God who made you and have cared for you. I will be your God throughout your entire life, even if your body is frail, your hair is white with age, the mind no longer functions like it once did and you can no longer care for yourself. I will remain your God and I will be with you (Isa. 46:3–4).

Chapter Fifteen

Warm welcomes, unconditional acceptance—
Sounds like the perfect friend. But what
does religion have to do with it?

A Faith-based Memorial for Annette's Pet? You Can't Be Serious!

I became a pet owner not by choice. It happened when my wife and children walked in with a cuddly six-week-old Keeshond puppy that would erase a frown off the face of the devil. I am one of upwards to 200 million people in America alone who have pets. I have known some who agree with the sentiments Lord Byron expressed in a tribute to Boatswain, his valued dog, as one

> Who possessed Beauty
> Without Vanity,
> Strength without Insolence,
> Courage without Ferocity,
> And all the virtues of Man
> Without his vices.[79]

Annette was one of them. By choice, she remained unmarried. Even though she appreciated her independence, Annette was surrounded by a battalion of friends who were developed in church, community, and workplace.

But one friend, Miki, a miniature terrier that weighed no more than fifteen pounds soaking wet, was around her more than others. I suppose that's the reason the dog meant so much to her. The pleasure

187

Miki brought was clear for anyone to see—extravagant exuberance, uninhibited welcome of a wagging tail, oodles of excitement on the return home from the office, unconditional acceptance, eagerness to provide protection (of questionable value, but the spirit was willing even though the flesh was weak!)—these made it easy to understand Annette's deep affection for her.

It probably wasn't unique to Miki, but she seemed to have an uncanny sixth sense when things weren't right. For example, during recovery from surgery and illnesses, she would jump on the bed, strictly forbidden under any other circumstances, and lay body-to-body with her head resting softly on Annette's arm.

I have seen other heart-warming indications of affection between owners and pets. One is the dachshund down the street that meant more than words can tell to Olivia after Mitch died. Also Chum-Chum whose pedigree was always suspicious. He enriched Charlie's life in more ways than anyone could count. And Roscoe, the cat of dubious heritage that added a special sense of caring to the Wilson family. Oh, I should not forget Bum, the God-knows-what-breed-of-a-dog whose face was so ugly that it could reduce a grown person to tears, but in other ways so outgoing, congenial, and lively that neighbors couldn't keep from loving him!

With age, Miki suffered from disabilities like blindness and arthritis, just like humans. But the straw that broke the camel's back was cancer. She was given proper care. But the time all too soon arrived that Annette had dreaded. A decision about Miki's life had to be made and the handwriting had been on the wall for some time. The conscientious, compassionate decision was to have her beloved pet put to sleep. For Annette, it was a serious matter—very serious.

I am not one who would let his feelings go as far as Pat O'Cotter when he penned:

> (It) would be a low-grade sort of Heaven,
> And I'd never regret a . . . sin,
> If I rush up to the gates white and pearly,
> And they don't let my male-mute in.[80]

But I fully appreciated and respected Annette's feelings. She asked if I would conduct some type of memorial as a tribute to her faithful friend of many years. "Am I being ridiculous?" she asked. The one that caused me deeper thought was, "Would it be Christian?" She felt awkward, maybe a bit embarrassed.

Should I?

Did I?

I'll come back to my response later. In the meanwhile,

Eight Guidebook Answers—on Behalf of the Doggie (or Whatever) in the Window . . . Owners, Too

1. Make a smart choice.

Select a pet that has a track record for being domesticated—does a big cat, reptile, or primate meet that requirement? Of course not! A lot of other creatures that are considered exotic are also unreasonable and could be dangerous. I have known about people who were injured, even killed, by animals they attempted to turn into pets. Only a few days ago, a person in America's northeast was viciously attacked by a neighbor's chimpanzee. Choose from those which pose the lowest possible risk to family members and others. It is unfair to everyone concerned, including the animal, to do otherwise.

2. Discount the care line.

Often children push the button of parents and grandparents to get a pet. In an effort to seal the deal, they make every promise known to the human race—and a few not yet known! One is as old as Methuselah: "Oh, please, get one! I'll take care of it!"

If the promise is actually kept, thank God for small miracles. The truth is, however, it usually lasts for seventy-two hours max. Therefore, at the time the decision is made to get a pet, be prepared to take care of it personally.

3. Show pleasure.

When a pet does something that brings enjoyment, return the favor. An owner who contacted me said that for him, it is simple since his Schnauzer is the easiest member of the family to please. He added, "A pat on the head, a cheerful word, or a stroke on the back is all it takes—thank God! Wish that were true for others in my house!"

A well-known trainer was adamant when she insisted, "No one should have as a pet any animal to which pleasure can't be shown personally or one which can't respond in a noticeable way."

Pets like Miki respond best to praise and excitement. In ways we probably don't fully understand, they pick up on the words, the spirit in which they are conveyed, and feelings of humans who are closest to them. According to the trainer, "That's the reason you need to show delight to your pet. And to do it with enthusiasm."

4. Rod and lollipop correction.

Pets are like children: They deserve to be corrected when needed, but not constantly, not excessively, and not when an owner is out of control. And just like it is with children, correction never means hateful treatment or brutality. Never! Cruelty to an animal should not be tolerated. Don't close your eyes or turn a deaf ear when animal abuse is going on. Report it! That is a responsible act by a believer on behalf of one of God's creations.

I mentioned the Rod and Lollipop System. It adds reward to correction, such as a treat for obedience. The system is more effective because it teaches the pet that "when you do this, you'll get that—something you like." Nothing garners attention like a treat; it is also simple and inexpensive.

5. Provide care *daily.*

I conducted an informal survey on-line among pet owners. The question was, "What is most important to you about having a pet?" I was surprised that hundreds of people replied with answers like:

"I must be the boss, not my pet."

"Never abuse the pet."

"Knowing where my pet is and what it is doing."

"Never taking my pet for granted."

"Being consistent and fair."

Quite a few mentioned the need to provide a "pet with the care it needs." Some went out of their way to remind me that care is a daily responsibility.

How many owners are guilty of the sin of Get and Forget—they get a pet then forget it after the newness wears off. "Well, it's only a dog," someone argued. A regular theme in the responses to my on-line question was this: Positive pet-hood is work and requires care. It includes fresh water and food each day, healthy diet (yes, it does make a difference), attention of a veterinarian when needed (animals get sick, too), exercise (most dogs love to walk and romp in a park), and moments of special attention. The animal trainer to whom I referred advised, "Anyone who does not have a moment here and there for a pet is too busy to have a pet."

6. Accept other responsibilities.

Depending on the pet, one responsibility is training. Do it or see that it is done. Whoever trains an animal should be qualified. If not, it will probably be a waste of time. But training includes more than pets. To become an effective owner, experts have told me, a master needs training as much as the pet, sometimes more than the pet! Find a trainer who serves both master and pet.

Another responsibility is the freedom for a pet to be a pet, nothing more or less than a pet. Some of the responses to my on-line question emphasized how important it is to remember "the pet is a pet, not a human." As in life, freedom for a pet has guidelines. Establish what the animal will be allowed to do. Be sure about what will not be permitted. As one of the responders stated, "Be fair and consistent."

Control is also a responsibility of the owner. Many animals, even domesticated ones, are territorial and will show aggression when they sense that their space is violated. It is ingrained in their make-up. Whatever is required, make sure that a pet is non-threatening to children, neighbors, and other animals.

And let's not forget cleanliness. The space a pet occupies needs to be kept tidy and sanitary. If a human doesn't accept the responsibility, who will? Dogs love exercise—and, like you and me, desperately need it. A natural bodily function usually occurs during walking and other forms of exercise. Be the kind of Christian you would like for others to be—clean up waste the animal leaves.

7. Use common sense and $$$ and cents.

How many pets should a person have? I realize that there are variables which have a bearing on the answer and that millions of families have more than one pet. Seldom, however, have I seen that more than one pet at a time to be a good idea or justified. I have observed that in families with several pets, the animals tend to suffer lack of attention. Besides, there is expense involved—$$$ and cents. More pets, more expense.

The average cost of care each year for cats and dogs is now $200 per family, according to the Humane Society with which I have contact. If use of available funds should be factored into ownership, it places limits on the amount that is reasonable to be allocated for pets. Budgeting and use of resources is a spiritual discipline that also applies to pets.

8. Think Pet—a gift from God.

A pet is a life.

A life requires creation.

At the root of creation is a creator.

In every form, life is so intricate, sophisticated, and marvelous that it takes something or someone bigger than life to make it happen.

Enter God!

PETS ARE GIFTS FROM GOD.
A PET IS GOD'S GIFT TO THE OWNER.

The gift concept introduces an exciting dimension to master-pet connection and behavior. A pet owner does himself and his pet a favor by reversing roles. For a moment, the pet is the owner with power to make choices and the owner is the pet.

Would the owner, as the pet, choose a master like the owner? Would the owner, as the pet, want to be treated in the way the pet has been treated? It is a Golden Rule of Pet-hood.

Now, back to Annette's request for some type of faith-based memorial in Miki's honor. Should I conduct one? Or would it be inappropriate, in fact, silly and a waste of valuable time (although the request was made with good intentions)? Maybe the idea should have been tossed aside as too non-spiritual. Animals don't possess awareness of soul or capacity for religious experience, do they? At least, not that we know.

What would you have done?

To me, the essential consideration was Annette. What would comfort and strengthen her? How valuable was Miki's contribution to her life? My response, "Yes, I'll do it."

A private Time of Tribute held in her garden began by outlining some ways pets bless people before I emphasized Miki's importance to Annette's life and God's compassionate nature for animals and supreme regard for the environment and all creation.

I was really glad that I led the tribute; I could see that Annette was blessed.

The few close friends she invited and I came away with a stronger awareness of God's goodness that includes bringing pets into the lives of people. Since then, others have agreed.

When I lead the morning prayer in my church on Sundays, I make it a point to avoid generic, rambling petitions to God. Instead, I zero in on a need in the congregation and community, like the ones included in this book. Not long ago, the focus of a prayer was pets, people with pets, and treatment of pets. Usually prayers in worship services create about as much stir as the wind on a sweltering summer day. But not the one about pets! I was shocked by the number of people who contacted me, not a one of whom took exception to the prayer. All expressed agreement—and gratitude.

Since God made animals, too, I would not at all be surprised if the Lord also agreed.

A. P. S.
(Author's Postscript)

Pet ownership in many nations, especially America and Canada, is significant. As I indicated, the number in America is up to 200 million representing a majority of households. It is a supplier's paradise. The money spent on upkeep has doubled in recent years. At the present pace, about $14 billion—*billion*—will be spent on pet care by year's end. That figures out to about $250 per dog and $200 per cat.

It isn't surprising that to a growing number of families, pets have become more than pets. They are like members of the family. When the family pet has a crisis, its shadow falls over the entire family. From ancient times, even the days of early pharaohs in Egypt, pets have been a source of enjoyment. But having one also involves serious responsibilities, thoughtful care, freedom with restraints, ordinary decency, firm limits, and the application of everyday horse sense. A faith-based approach is also important.

Discussion Room

Agree	Disagree	
☐	☐	A pet owner should treat his or her pet in the way he or she would like to be treated.
☐	☐	Time taken up with pets is silly. It isn't the best use of time
☐	☐	God created pets.
☐	☐	With so many needy people in the community, money spent on pets should be used to help people with needs.
☐	☐	It's wrong to buy and sell animals.
☐	☐	My church has more important causes to address than pet care.
☐	☐	Putting a pet to death is okay when health issues indicate it is the compassionate thing to do.

Agree	Disagree	
☐	☐	Pets should be kept outdoors.
☐	☐	Pets will be in heaven.
☐	☐	Faith should have a positive impact on treatment of animals, the environment, and all creation.
☐	☐	There isn't enough reliable information available to make global warming a hot button issue.
☐	☐	Environmentalists are fanatics.
☐	☐	If protection of the environment and animals is detrimental to humans, the interests of humans come first.
☐	☐	Believers aren't shouldering their share of the load in environmental issues.
☐	☐	Save souls—not tigers.
☐	☐	Development of all sources of energy is mandated by faith, in addition to reasons like energy independence and national security.
☐	☐	The primary role of government in global warming, the polar ice cap, conservation, and development of all sources for energy is the well-being of its citizens.
☐	☐	The God of heaven should also be honored as the Lord of the earth.

Eight Leading No-No's for Pet Owners According to Pet Owners I've Known

- Mistreatment—"failure to practice a Golden Rule for pets" ... "Violent reactions" ... "Brutality" ... "Non-violent abuse such as verbal"

- Insufficient attention—"inadequate time given to the pet for activities like exercise and socialization"
- Lack of stimulation—"a pet needs challenges"
- Failure to train—"they have to know what is expected of them—it comes through training, effective training, to which they can respond" . . . "if training is not successful the first time, have a do over" . . . "use a trainer who gets the job done with the pet AND owner"
- Loss of interest—"at first, a pet may be lots of fun and get attention (maybe too much attention), but over time, fun and attention fade away"
- Insignificance—"a low life concept of animal life—the idea that creatures can be treated any way a human wants to treat them"
- Isolation—"leave them alone too much and for too long" . . . "failure to arrange for care when away"
- No authority—"the owner doesn't say what he means, doesn't mean what he says, and doesn't mean what he does" (example, offer a treat to reward the pet for obedience, but animal gets no treat)

Prayer for Pet Owners—Creation—Environment

Wise and creative God, You give life and breath to everything that is.

Birds of the air, fish in the sea, squirrels in the trees, noisy geese which make a home out of a stopover in their migration, the tiny creatures which have no apparent purpose and for which existence is measured in hours, not years, not even days, and pets to bless humans.

Everything! Great and small! How majestic are Your ways!

You are behind the life of animals like Miki just as much as You are for any of us.

Lord of life, help owners to recognize that pets deserve proper care. Come inside them to renew a caring spirit. Help them to think of pets as gifts that You have brought into their lives.

Grant them, and everyone, a stronger appreciation for all life. And walk alongside them supplying wisdom to make decisions which benefit the environment and Your creation. In the name of Him to whom all life is valuable. Amen.

Good News

How many are your works, O Lord. In wisdom, you made them all; the earth is full of your creatures . . . living things both large and small (Ps. 104:24).

Chapter Sixteen

Last Word: Thanks—Rise!

For a long time, I have made it my business to read what others write and listen to what they have to say. Occasionally, I have disagreed with them. At times, I took exception to much of what I heard. However, early on I found that if they caused me to think, challenged me do something positive, and, in commitment as a follower of Jesus Christ, prompted me to go deeper and further, then the time spent was useful.

You may not agree with everything I have written. If the truth were known, you may disagree with much of what you have read. You may see some issues from a different perspective and approach answers from another angle. But if I have caused you to think at least for a moment, if I have challenged you to make an effort to solve some problems and be a problem solver instead of a problem, if your desire has heated up a degree or two to try and make a difference in your family, church, community, and workplace, if your heart has been warmed again to pray for someone with a need, and if you have been pushed toward a more dynamic commitment to the Heavenly Father, then I will consider my efforts to have been worthwhile.

Thanks for allowing me to come alongside you through these pages.

Jesus said, "Rise, let's go from this place" (Matt. 26:46). To me, that is one of the most revealing phrases about Jesus ever spoken. Death stared him in the face. And His followers were about to fail him miserably. In a matter of minutes, they would run away and forsake Him—every last one of them.

Soon, Peter, one of the main disciples, would curse as he vehemently denied that he ever knew the Galilean. As a practical matter and applied to everyday life, the words Jesus spoke mean:

- You are where you are
- You don't have to remain where you are
- It's possible for you to get to where you could (and should) be
- You can get there—where you could and should be—from here, where you are.

I have started work on the second book in this series. It opens readers into the lives of some amazing people who have influenced my life in extraordinary ways. One is Norman who got from where he was—an average, small town kid—to chief of surgery at one of America's leading medical centers. And Arnold, who rose from the bottom of the heap to head the biggest financial company of its kind without stepping on a single person. During the climb, he pulled a lot of people with him. I wouldn't dare leave out Layne, the humble supermarket manager, whose "no" saved my life.

Or Randi (professional name)—oh, dear Randi—who ran away from home when barely a teenager, lived and worked on the streets, started coming to her senses, and became a child of transformation. Against every odd known to human kind, she completed high school, graduated from college, married, and mothers a family that would make anyone stand up and cheer.

One formerly known as "Randi" discovered that she could get there—her Land of Could And Should Be—from here—where she was, wherever it was.

So can you.

I imagine God is nodding in agreement.

Until our paths cross again—rise to your possibilities.

Endnotes

1. Hall, Hattie Vose. *Two Temples*. Retrieved February 17, 2008 from http://www.poeticportal.net/content/view/875/291.
2. Barrie, James M. *Dairy*. Retrieved April 7, 2008 as a Classic Quote from http://www.quotations.com.
3. Lowell, James Russell. *Children Are*. Retrieved February 17, 2008 from http://www.giga-usa.com/quotes/authors/james_russell_lowell_aO.
4. Woodworth, Samuel. *The Old Wooden Bucket* (as censored by Board of Health). Author of censored version unknown.
5. American Psychological Association. *Understanding Child Sexual Abuse*. Retrieved February 17, 2008 from http://www.APA.com.
6. Ibid.
7. Hopper, Jim. *Sexual Abuse of Males*. Retrieved February 17, 2008 from http://jimhopper.com.
8. Ibid.
9. Ibid.
10. Osborne, David, M.D. Special to CNN. Retrieved February 18, 2008 from http://www.mayoclinic.com.

11. American Psychological Association, *Sexual Orientation & Homosexuality*. Retrieved February 17, 2008 from http://www. APA.com.
12. Felleman, Hazel. Best Loved Poems. *The Woman I Am*, Glen Allen. Garden City, NJ, Doubleday & Company, 1936.
13. Eitsen, D. Stanley. Sociology. *The Atrophy of Social Life* (Dubuque, IA, McGraw-Hill, 2006).
14. Levine, Robert V. Sociology. *The Kindness of Strangers* (Dubuque, IA, McGraw-Hill, 2006).
15. *Statistics On Homosexuality*. Retrieved April 24, 2008 from http://www.catholicintl.com/news.htm.
16. Ibid.
17. Ibid.
18. *Martin Luther Encyclopedia*. Retrieved April 28, 2008 from http://www.iep.utm.edi/l/luther.htm.
19. *Statistics On Homosexuality*. Retrieved April 24, 2008 from http://www.catholiclicintl.com/news.htm.
20. *Charity*. Author unknown. Retrieved October 17, 2008 from http://www.my.opera.com/Over_and_over/index.dml/tag.
21. Dr. Paul Cameron. Institute for Scientific Investigation of Sexuality. Retrieved April 28, 2008 from http://www.afec.org/issues.htm.
22. Dr. Joseph Nicolosi. National Association For Psychoanalytic Research and Therapy. Retrieved April 28, 2008 from http://www.afec.org/issues.htm.
23. *Statistics On Homosexuality*. Retrieved April 28, 2008 from http://www.afec.org/issues.htm.
24. Ontario Consultants On Religious Tolerance. Retrieved May 4, 2008 from http://www.religioustolerance.org.
25. Information source. http://freerepublic.com/focus/news/1502263.
26. Gay, John. *The Beggar's Opera*. Retrieved May 16, 2008 from http://www.wikipedia.org.wiki/The_Beggar's_Opera.
27. Cherlin, Andrew. John Hopkins University. From the Washington Post (Staleup).
28. *Cohabitation Facts*. Retrieved May 22, 2008 from http://www.members.aol.com/cohabiting/facts.htm.

29. Ibid.

30. Ibid.

31. Seltzer & Teachman. *The Problem of Cohabitation*. Retrieved May 10, 2008 from http://www.members.aol.com/cohabiting/facts.htm.

32. *Cohabitation Facts*. Retrieved April 22, 2008 from http://www.members.aol.com/cohabiting/facts.htm.

33. Ibid.

34. Seltzer & Teachman. *The Problem of Cohabitation*. Retrieved May 10, 2008 from http://www.members.aol.com/cohabiting/intro.htm.

35. Albuquerque, NM Journal, December 2, 2007.

36. Rose, Gary L. Medical Institute for Sexual Health. Article in Washington Times, December 6, 2007.

37. Vanden Bergh, Bea R.H. and Marcoen, Alfons. *Child Development* (2004). Retrieved from http://www.medscape.com.

38. Information source http://www.nrlc.org/euthanasia/asisend3.html.

39. *Albert Schweitzer Quotes*. Retrieved May 6, 2008 from http://www.brainyquotes.com/quotes/authors/a/albertschweitzer.

40. Information retrieved January 23, 2007 from https://j.ovm1.net/ahp1/effexor.htm.

41. Dr. David Clark. Retrieved January 23, 2007 from http://www.psychologyinfo.com.htm.

42. Information from American Journal of Psychiatry retrieved January 23, 2008 from http://www.psychologyinfo.com/depression.htm.

43. Final Report of the Attorney General's Commission On Pornography. Michael McManus, ed. Rutledge Hill Press, Nashville, TN.

44. *Dear Abby*. The Clarion-Ledger, Jackson, MS. May 16, 2008.

45. Zillman, Dolf and Bryant, Jennings. *Pornography, Sexual Callousness, and Trivialization of Rape*, Journal of Communications 32/15.

46. Harley, Willard F. *Coping With Infidelity*. Retrieved August 2, 2008 from http://www.marriagebuilders.com.

47. Powel, Blaine. *Affairs*. Retrieved August 2, 2008 from http://www.ca/counseling/resources/factsheets/affairs.php.

48. Vaughan, Peggy. *Who Has Affairs—And Why?* Retrieved May 21, 2008 from http://www.adulthoodwonderful.com/survive.htm.
49. Ibid.
50. McGraw, Phil. *Dr. Phil's Advice About Affairs.* Retrieved May 22, 2008 from http://www.oprah.com.
51. Harley, Willard F. *Coping With Infidelity.* Retrieved August 2, 2008 from http://www.marriagebuilders.com.
52. McGraw, Phil. *Dr. Phil's Advice About Affairs.* Retrieved May 22, 2008 from http:/www.oprah.com.
53. Lewis, C. S. *Mere Christianity.* Geoffrey Bles, Ltd., London, England.
54. *Suicide Prevention Scientific Information.* Center For Disease Control. Retrieved September 11, 2008 from http://www.cdc.gov/ncipc/dvp/suicide-conque.
55. From Richelieu, Act II, sc. 2.
56. 16th century rhyme. Retrieved October 10, 2008 from http://www.rhymes.org.uk.humpty-dumpty.htm.
57. King, Martin Luther. *Faith.* Retrieved October 11, 2008 from http://www.brainyquote.com/quotes/authors/m/martin_luther_king.
58. American Association of Suicidology. Retrieved October 11, 2008 from http://www.suicidology.org.
59. Ibid.
60. *Suicide, Facts At A Glance – Fatal Suicidal Behavior.* Retrieved October 6, 2008 from http://www.cdc.gov/injury.
61. Mayo Foundation For Education and Research. *Medical Information.* Retrieved May 23, 2008 from http://www.mayoclinic.com.
62. Hudibras (part 1, canto III, 1.878).
63. Evans, Patricia. *The Verbally Abusive Relationship.* Retrieved July 10, 2008 from http://www.patriciaevans.com.
64. *Michelangelo Quotes.* Retrieved June 6, 2008 from http://www.quotation page.com/36775.html.
65. Galanter, Marc, M.D. Director of Alcoholism and Drug Abuse, New York University Medical Center. In a letter published by *Dear Abby*, the Clarion-Ledger, April 28,2008. Universal Press Syndicate.
66. Published by Rand McNally Company. Copyright W.B. Conkey Company. Retrieved April 20, 2008 from http://shelbyjackman.com/school/timeline/1850-1854.html.

67. *Straight Facts About Drugs and Alcohol.* Retrieved July 6, 2008 from http://www.ncadi.samhsa.gov/govpubs/rp0884.
68. Ibid.
69. *Robinson, Corinne Roosevelt.* The Path That Leads To Nowhere. *Retrieved May 9, 2008 from http://www.daypoems.net/poems/1384. html.*
70. Retrieved May 17, 2008 from http:/www./healthline.com.
71. Ibid.
72. Ibid.
73. Fletcher, Louisa. Land of Beginning Again. Retrieved May 19, 2008 from *http://www.uvachurch.com/articles_The Land Of Beginning Again.com.*
74. Retrieved May 17, 2008 from http://www.healthline.com.
75. Ibid.
76. Ibid.
77. U.S. Census Bureau/National Center For Health Statistics. Retrieved April 20, 2008 from http://www.census.gov/population/socdemo/marr-div.html.
78. National Institute Of Health. Retrieved March 17, 2008 from http://nimh.nih.gov.html.
79. Whitmer, Rachel. Belly May Signal Later Dementia. Jackson, MS Clarion-Ledger. March 27, 2007.
80. Ibid.
81. Lord Byron. *A Memorial To Boatswain.* JG Publishing Company. Retrieved April 21, 2008 from http://readytogoebooks.com/LB_dog_p63.html.
82. Pat O'Cotter. A Malemute Dog. Retrieved April 21, 2008 from http://www-hsc.usc.edu/cypert/inheaven.html.

Diligent effort has been made to locate and acknowledge the sources of all copyrighted materials used. If any acknowledgments have been inadvertently omitted or errors made, the author would appreciate receiving full information so that proper credit may be given in subsequent printings.